CULTURE AND CUSTOMS
OF THE PALESTINIANS

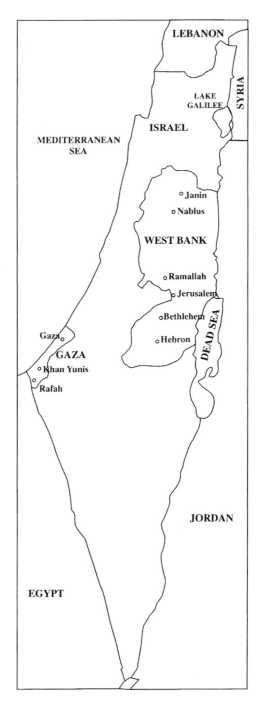

Figure 1.1
Historic Palestine with Israel and the Occupied
Palestinian Territories. Cartography by Book-
comp, Inc.

CULTURE AND CUSTOMS
OF THE PALESTINIANS

Samih K. Farsoun

Culture and Customs of the Middle East

GREENWOOD PRESS
Westport, Connecticut • London

Library of Congress Cataloging-in-Publication Data

Farsoun, Samih K.
  Culture and customs of the Palestinians / Samih K. Farsoun.
    p. cm. — (Culture and customs of the Middle East, ISSN 1550–1310)
  Includes bibliographical references and index.
  ISBN 0–313–32051–9 (hardcover : alk. paper)
  1. Ethnology—Palestine. 2. Palestine—Social life and customs.
  I. Title. II. Series.
  GN635.P19F37   2004
  306'.095694—dc22   2004014141

British Library Cataloguing in Publication Data is available.

Library of Congress Catalog Card Number: 2004014141
ISBN: 0–313–32051–9
ISSN: 1550–1310

First published in 2004

Greenwood Press, 88 Post Road West, Westport, CT 06881
An imprint of Greenwood Publishing Group, Inc.
www.greenwood.com

Printed in the United States of America

The paper used in this book complies with the
Permanent Paper Standard issued by the National
Information Standards Organization (Z39.48–1984).

10   9   8   7   6   5   4   3   2   1

To the memory of my mother, Marie, and to my sisters, Regina, Despina, and Samia, all of whom taught me much about the traditional culture of Palestine.

To my wife, Katha, who taught me always to look to the future.

To my daughter, Rouwayda, that she may learn and remember her heritage.

Contents

Series Foreword

At last! *Culture and Customs of the Middle East* fills a deep void in reference literature by providing substantial individual volumes on crucial countries in the explosive region. The series is available at a critical juncture, with, among other events, the recent war on Iraq, the continued wrangling by U.S. interests for control of regional oil resources, the quest for Palestinian independence and justice for the refugees, and the spread of religious fundamentalist violence and repression. The authoritative, objective, and engaging cultural overviews complement and balance the volley of news bites.

As with the other Culture and Customs series, the narrative focus is on contemporary culture and life, in a historical context. Each volume is written for students and general readers by a country expert. Contents include, where relevant,

Chronology

Context, including land, people, and brief historical overview

Religion and world view

Literature

Media

Cinema

Art and architecture/housing

Cuisine and dress

Gender, marriage, and family

Social customs and lifestyle

Acknowledgments

I want to thank the many people and institutions whose help was essential in writing this book. The American University Library and the Library of the Palestine Center, Washington, D.C., were important sources of research materials for writing this book.

I am also grateful for the assistance of a number of individuals who assisted with or contributed to this project. They include Natalie Hand, who helped in researching and initially drafting the section on Palestinian novelists. Similarly, Brock Bevan helped with research on Palestinian films and filmmakers. I also want to thank Salim Fahmawi of the United Nations on Palestinian costumes and Heidi Shoup and Executive Director Nadia Hijab for assistance and for facilitating my work at the Palestine Center. The staff of the Palestine Center, Jeff Mendez, Samar Assad, Casey Riley, and Tareq Bremer, offered much help in numerous ways that made the writing of this book much easier and more pleasant. My sincere thanks go to all of them. I wish to thank my friends and colleagues, Professors Naseer Aruri, Chancellor Professor Emeritus, University of Massachusetts, and Cheryl Rubenberg, previously of Florida International University, for the help, advice, and support they both extended to me.

I want to thank Ms. Wendi Schnaufer of Greenwood Press for her patience and constant support throughout the stages of this project.

Finally, my special thanks go to my wife, Katha Kissman, whose consistent help, constant encouragement, and unwavering support made possible the completion of this book.

In the end, those who helped bear no blame for any errors, interpretations, or conclusions in this book. Those are my responsibility.

Preface

The Palestinians have been at the center of Middle Eastern and world history for nearly a century. More United Nations resolutions have been passed regarding the question of Palestine and the derivative Arab-Israeli conflict than any other issue. Peace and war, stability and instability in the Middle East region and political tension in the world have most often revolved around the question of Palestine and the Palestinians. Also, no political and diplomatic issue has received so many "peace plans" by so many U.S. Presidents and Secretaries of State as the Palestine conflict. Because the circumstances and destiny of the Palestinians are of significant concern to the Arab and Muslim peoples and states, the dilemma of Palestine and the Palestinians has had more international focus than any other issue since World War II. Even the Cold War occasionally took a backseat to the conflict over Palestine and the struggles of its people. While the demise of Communism led to the end of the Cold War, the Palestine question remains unresolved and seemingly more intractable and more volatile than ever.

The struggle of the Palestinians against the draconian Israeli occupation appears almost daily in the news. The core issues of the Palestinian-Israeli conflict are still the issues that emerged in 1948 after the catastrophe of the destruction of Palestine and the dispossession and expulsion of its people. Complicating this original conundrum is the Israeli occupation of the remaining parts of historic Palestine (the West Bank and the Gaza Strip) in 1967 and its illegal actions in the occupied territories. The outstanding unresolved issues of the question of Palestine include ending the Israeli occupation of the Palestinian territories, the status of Jerusalem, the illegal Israeli settlements in the occupied territories, the separation Wall on Palestinian land, and the establishment of a sovereign Palestinian state in all of the West Bank and Gaza with its capital in (east) Jerusalem.

While these latter problems emerged as a result of Israeli actions during the long occupation of the West Bank and Gaza Strip (since the Arab-Israeli war of 1967) and have taken center stage, the issues that emerged after 1948 also have not been resolved. In particular, these include the right of return of Palestinian refugees to their homeland, articulated in UN resolutions and international law, and their right to compensation and reparations.

In late March 2004, the Palestinian-Israeli conflict took a turn for the worse as Israel assassinated a highly respected spiritual leader (a quadriplegic religious cleric), Sheik Ahmed Yassin of Hamas, one of the Palestinian political factions resisting the occupation. Hamas, an Islamist political movement, burst into the news in the 1990s as a result of its unorthodox use of suicide bombings, especially from among the desperate Gaza Strip Palestinians, as part of its fight against the Israeli occupation. Although the Western news media cover widely and extensively the stories of suicide bombings and their victims, the same media do not match this with coverage of the Israeli military's outrages against the Palestinian people nor the long and oppressive occupation that is the source of the currently uncivil, violent conflict.

At the center of all this vortex of politics, diplomacy, oppression, suppression, resistance, and struggle are the Palestinian people. An ancient people with strong ties to their land and with deeply rooted customs and traditions, the Palestinians have not disappeared in the wake of their tragedy in 1948, neither have they yielded to defeat nor to the loss of their homeland. This book provides a general overview of the culture and the customs of the Palestinians set in the historical context of their defining experience: *al-Nakba*, Arabic for "catastrophe," the word with which the Palestinians themselves define and describe the destruction of their society in 1948, the dispossession and expulsion of most of its people as stateless refugees, and their destitution at the hands of the Israelis. The Palestinians, who now number around nine million people, have persevered, even flourished, asserted their identity, preserved but also transformed and modernized their traditional culture, both inside historic Palestine and in the diaspora.

This book comprises seven chapters covering the historical context of Palestine and the Palestinians, Palestinian society and customs, patterns of marriage, the family and gender, their unique traditional dress and costumes and their cuisine, their religions and religious customs, and their culture. The last two chapters describe and review Palestinian literature, music, dance, art, and performing arts, as well as the new art and craft of cinematography. The book also includes an extensive chronology, a glossary of Palestinian Arabic terms, and an essential bibliography for reference and research.

Chronology

A.D. 661–750	Palestine becomes a province under the Arab-Islamic Umayyad Dynasty, which was based in Damascus.
685–91	The Ummayad Caliph Abdul Malik Ibn Marwan (685–705) builds the Dome of the Rock in Jerusalem.
705	Al-Walid Ibn Abdul Malik (705–15) of the Umayyads builds Al-Aqsa Mosque in Jerusalem.
750–1258	Palestine becomes a province under the Arab-Islamic Abbasid Dynasty based in Baghdad.
1099–1187	The Crusaders invade Palestine and establish the Latin Kingdom of Jerusalem.
1187	The Battle of Hittin in Palestine. Saladin of Egypt defeats the Crusaders and liberates Palestine from European Crusader control. Palestine is re-Arabized and re-Islamized.
1517	Ottoman conquest of most of the Arab World, including Palestine.
1517–1918	Palestine under Ottoman rule.
1882–1904	First wave of immigration of Jewish settlers to Palestine.
1897	First Zionist Congress meets in Basel, Switzerland. The Basel Program is launched to settle Jews in Palestine and the World Zionist Organization is established.
1904–14	Second wave of immigration of Jewish settlers to Palestine.

1911	*Filistine* newspaper is founded in Jaffa by Issa al-Issa. The newspaper addresses Arabs in Palestine as Palestinians, warning them of the consequences of the Zionist colonization of Palestine.
1915–16	Sharif Hussein and Henry McMahon, the British high commissioner in Egypt, exchange correspondence guaranteeing Arab independence in return for the Arab revolt against the Ottomans.
1916	
16 May	Britain and France sign the secret Sykes-Picot Agreement, which divides the Ottoman Arab provinces among them.
1917	
2 November	Lord Arthur James Balfour, British foreign secretary, sends a letter (later known as the Balfour Declaration) to Lord Edmund de Rothschild supporting the establishment of a Jewish national home in Palestine.
1918	
9 December	British forces occupy Palestine.
1919	First National Conference–Palestine; the U.S. King-Crane Commission.
1920	
24 April	San Remo Conference grants Great Britain mandate over Palestine.
1922	
24 July	Council of the League of Nations Mandate for Palestine.
1936–39	Arab revolt erupts in Palestine.
1937	
7 July	The Peel Commission Report recommends turning Palestine into a Jewish State and an Arab State incorporated into Transjordan, with Jerusalem and Bethlehem placed under the British Mandate.
1939	
17 May	The British government issues the MacDonald White Paper to limit and restrict Jewish immigration and land purchases in Palestine.

1942

11 May	The Zionists attending the Biltmore Conference in New York advocate the establishment of a "Jewish Commonwealth" in Palestine.
1946–48	Jewish-Palestinian-British war breaks out inside Palestine.

1947

29 November	Without consultation with Palestinians, the United Nations Special Committee on Palestine recommends the Partition of Palestine (UN General Assembly Resolution 181) into an Arab state and a Jewish state and that Jerusalem and its environs be internationalized.

1948

9 April	Jewish underground forces, the Irgun and Stern gangs, massacre 254 Palestinians in the village of Deir Yassin near Jerusalem.
14 May	The mandate over Palestine officially ends, and the Zionist political leadership proclaims the establishment of the state of Israel. The United States extends full diplomatic recognition to Israel. The Soviet Union follows suit. Palestine is dismembered, and most of its population is expelled to becomes refugees in neighboring Arab countries and in the West Bank and Gaza Strip, which remain in Arab hands and behind military lines.
1 September	The Palestinian National Conference meets in Gaza, and the All-Palestine Government is established under the leadership of Hajj Amin al-Husseini. Al-Husseini heads the meeting of the Palestinian National Council in Gaza.
1 December	Palestinian notables from east-central Palestine, the area that remained under Jordanian military control (and later called the West Bank), meet in Jericho and advocate a temporary union with Transjordan.
11 December	The United Nations General Assembly adopts Resolution 194, which recognizes the right of Palestinians who were expelled by the Israeli army or who fled during the 1948 war to return to their homes. A condition that the United Nations also set for accepting Israel as a member of the United Nations.
1949	At the end of the 1948 war, Israel extends its holdings of Palestine and controls 78 percent rather than the 56 percent allo-

	cated by the UN Partition Plan of 1947 by conquering areas allotted by the United Nations to the Palestinian state.
12 August	Geneva Convention provides protection to civilians in time of war (Fourth Geneva Convention).
8 December	The United Nations announces the establishment of the United Nations Relief and Works Agency (UNRWA) to assist Palestinian refugees in the West Bank, Gaza Strip, Jordan, Syria, and Lebanon. The West Bank comes under Jordanian control, and Egypt asserts authority over Gaza.

1950

24 April	The West Bank officially becomes part of the Hashemite Kingdom of Jordan. The move is recognized by two states only: the United Kingdom and Pakistan.

1953

28 February	Israel launches a large-scale assault on the Gaza Strip.

1956

28–29 October	The Suez war (the second Arab-Israeli war). Israel invades and occupies the Gaza Strip and the Sinai Peninsula in preparation for a British-French invasion of Egypt to reinstate western control of the Suez.
1957	In Kuwait, Yasser 'Arafat, among others, founds the Palestine Liberation Movement, later renamed Fateh, which means "opening."

1964

28 May	Ahmed Shuqeiri, the Palestinian representative to the Arab League, heads the Palestinian National Council (PNC) meeting in Jerusalem, where the first Palestine Liberation Organization (PLO) National Covenant is drafted. At the PNC meeting, he is appointed the first chairman of the PLO.
2 June	The PLO is officially founded.

1967

5 June	Israel launches an attack that starts the June War, which lasts six days and is referred to as the Six Day War in Israel and the West; Israel captures East Jerusalem and the West Bank from Jordan and the Gaza Strip from Egypt as well as the Sinai Peninsula and the Golan Heights.
22 November	The United Nations Security Council adopts Resolution 242, which states that Israel must withdraw from territories occu-

pied during the Six Day War of 1967 in return for peace and secure borders. Israel does not.

11 December	George Habash establishes the Popular Front for the Liberation of Palestine. Israel annexes East Jerusalem and begins construction of Jewish settlements in East Jerusalem and the West Bank.

1968

21 March	The Battle of al-Karameh takes place in the village Karameh, east of the Jordan River, where Palestinian guerillas join the Jordanian army in resisting an Israeli military incursion into the East Bank.
17–18 July	The Palestinian National Council moves its headquarters to Cairo and amends the PLO's National Charter.

1970

September	PLO-Jordanian power struggle and civil war in Jordan. During this year, the Jordanian army launches an attack against Palestinian camps and guerillas on the outskirts of the Jordanian capital, Amman. The high Palestinian death toll in the attack is labeled "Black September" by the Palestinian movement.

1971

9 July	The Jordanian army evicts the PLO from Jordan and dismantles its infrastructure.
28 November	Black September, a Palestinian organization formed after the civil war between the PLO and Jordan in September 1970, claims responsibility for the assassination of Wasfi al-Tal, Jordan's Prime Minister.

1973

6 October	The October war breaks out when Syria and Egypt launch a coordinated attack on Israeli forces occupying the Golan Heights and the Sinai desert.
22 October	The United Nations Security Council adopts Resolution 338, recommending negotiations between Israel and its Arab neighbors.

1974

19 February	The Palestinian National Council accepts the establishment of a Palestinian state in any liberated part of Palestine and discards the established option or proposal of establishing a secular democratic state in all of Palestine to include Palestinian Muslims and Christians and Israeli Jews.

| 14 October | The United Nations General Assembly passes Resolution 3326, which accepts the PLO as the representative of the Palestinian people and grants them permanent observer status. PLO Chairman Yasser 'Arafat addresses the General Assembly in a famous speech. |

| 28 October | The Seventh Arab League Summit in Rabat recognizes the PLO as the sole legitimate representative of the Palestinian people. |

| 19 November | Egyptian President Anwar Sadat visits Israel and addresses the Israeli Knesset parliament. |

1978

| 14 March | The Israeli army invades southern Lebanon, demolishes a number of villages, and kills some 700 Lebanese and Palestinians. |

| 17 September | U.S. President Jimmy Carter, Egyptian President Anwar Sadat, and Israeli Prime Minister Menachem Begin sign the Camp David Accords. Israel agrees to withdraw from Sinai in exchange for peace with Egypt and to grant the Palestinians "full autonomy" in the Occupied Territories after a transitional period of five years. |

1979

| 22 March | The United Nations Security Council adopts Resolution 446, which demands that Israel dismantle the settlements in the Occupied Territories. |

| **1980** | The Israeli Knesset officially adopts the Jerusalem Law, which annexes East Jerusalem to Israel. |

1982

| 4 June | The Israeli army invades Lebanon to destroy the military, political, and institutional infrastructure of the PLO. Israel besieges Beirut for three months. Palestinian and Lebanese casualties were estimated at tens of thousands of people. The United States brokers an agreement for the withdrawal of Palestinian fighters from Beirut. |

| 16–18 September | Members of the Phalange militia allowed by the Israeli military enter the camps of Sabra and Shatila near Beirut, Lebanon, and massacre up to 2,000 Palestinian refugees. Later Defense Minister Ariel Sharon is held indirectly responsible for the massacre by an Israeli Court. The PLO sets up it headquarters in Tunis, Tunisia. |

1983

14–21 February   The Palestinian National Council meets in Algiers and approves the concept of a confederation between an independent Palestine and Jordan.

20 December   Chairman Yasser 'Arafat and 4,000 PLO commandos leave north Lebanon on Greek ships.

1984

28 February   Palestinians from the Occupied Territories meet PLO Chairman Yasser 'Arafat in Amman, Jordan, to urge him to accept a joint PLO and Jordanian strategy based on United Nations Security Council resolutions 242 and 338.

1985–87   The "war of the camps" in which Lebanese Amal (Shia) militias vent their hostility against PLO loyalists and Palestinian civilians, killing many refugees and destroying camps in Lebanon. The Syrian army, the deterrent force in the Lebanese civil war, looks the other way.

1985

11 February   PLO Chairman Yasser 'Arafat and Jordan's King Hussein agree on a formula for a joint Jordanian-Palestinian peace strategy.

19 November   The PLO Executive Committee meets in Baghdad and reaffirms the PLO's rejection of UN resolutions 242 and 338.

1986

19 February   King Hussein ends joint peace efforts with the PLO.

1987

9 December   The Palestinian *intifada* (uprising) begins in Gaza and spreads to the West Bank.

1988

16 April   Khalil al-Wazir (Abu Jihad), a PLO military leader, is assassinated in his home in Tunis.

31 July   King Hussein officially breaks administrative and legal ties with the West Bank and announces that he is relinquishing control to the PLO.

3 August   The PLO declares full responsibility for the affairs of the West Bank and Gaza.

24 November   The Palestinian National Council proclaims an independent Palestinian state in the West Bank and Gaza; 55 countries,

including China and the Soviet Union, recognize the Palestinian state.

7 December	Chairman Yasser 'Arafat declares in Stockholm that the PLO accepts Israel's right to exist and denounces terrorism. The United States rejects the term "denounce" and insists that he "renounces" terrorism.
14 December	The United States authorizes its ambassador to Tunis, Robert Pelletreau, to open a diplomatic dialogue with the PLO.

1989

12 January	The UN Security Council grants the PLO the right to speak directly to the council as "Palestine" with the same status as any UN member nation.
2 April	The PLO Central Council appoints the organization's chairman, Yasser 'Arafat, the first president of Palestine.
20 April	The UN General Assembly condemns Israeli practices in the Occupied Territories and calls on the UN Security Council to protect Palestinian civilians.

1990

9 April	Hamas issues its conditions for joining the PLO, requesting 40 percent of the Palestinian National Council's seats. Chairman Yasser 'Arafat rejects the request.
25 May	After the United States refuses to grant PLO Chairman Yasser 'Arafat a visa to enter New York to address the UN General Assembly, the assembly moves to Geneva, where 'Arafat calls for deployment of UN forces into the West Bank and Gaza.

1991

August	Iraq invades and occupies Kuwait
17 January	The United States and its allies attack Iraq, forcing it to withdraw from Kuwait. The United States emerges as the sole power broker in the region and plans to launch a new peace initiative in the region labeled the "peace process."
21 July	U.S. Secretary of State James Baker informs Palestinian leaders that the American initiative envisions the creation of "less than a state, and more than autonomy."
28 August	The PLO agrees, with provisions, to participate in the Middle East Peace Conference.

| 16 October | The PLO and Jordan agree to form a joint Jordanian-Palestinian delegation to attend the forthcoming Conference in Madrid. |
| 30 October | The Madrid peace conference begins with representatives from Israel, Egypt, Syria, Lebanon, Jordan, and Palestine. |

1993

30 August	The Norwegian government confirms that 14 rounds of secret talks were held in Norway between Israeli and Palestinian negotiators.
13 September	Mahmoud Abbas (Abu Mazen), spokesperson for the PLO Foreign Affairs Department and member of the PLO Executive Committee, and Israeli Foreign Minister Shimon Peres initial the Declaration of Principles (DOP). PLO Chairman Yasser 'Arafat and Israeli Prime Minister Yitzhak Rabin sign the accords and shake hands on the lawn of the White House.
19 September	The United States promises $250 million to the Palestinians to support the agreement. The Israeli Knesset approves the DOP 61 to 50.
12 October	The PLO establishes the Palestinian Authority (PA) and appoints 'Arafat its head.

1994

4 May	PLO Chairman Yasser 'Arafat and Israeli Prime Minister Yitzhak Rabin sign the Gaza-Jericho Self-Rule Accord (also known as the Cairo Agreement).
11 May	The Knesset approves the Gaza-Jericho Accord by a 52–0 vote.
26 June	The PA holds its first meeting in Gaza City.
1 July	'Arafat, accompanied and followed by a large part of the PLO bureaucracy, returns to Gaza triumphantly.
26 October	Israel and Jordan sign a peace treaty.
10 December	President 'Arafat, Prime Minister Rabin, and Israeli Foreign Minister Shimon Peres accept the Nobel Peace Prize.

1995

| 13 January | PA Minister of Planning and International Coordination Nabil Sha'ath announces that the PA has committed itself to peaceful resistance. |
| 28 September | PLO Chairman Yasser 'Arafat and Israeli Prime Minister Yitzhak Rabin sign the Palestinian-Israeli Interim Agreement |

	on the West Bank and Gaza Strip (Oslo II) at the White House.

9 November   Rabin is assassinated by Israeli law student, Yigal Amir.

1996

20 January   Elections are held for the PA presidency and the Palestinian Legislative Council. PLO Chairman Yasser 'Arafat wins the presidency with 88.1 percent of the vote.

4 May   'Arafat and the Palestine National Council amend the PLO National Charter, removing the call for the destruction of Israel.

2 June   Binyamin Netanyahu becomes Israel's Prime Minister.

1997

15 January   Israel and the PLO sign the Protocol Concerning the Redeployment in Hebron (the Hebron Agreement).

21 October   Israel's former Prime Minister Shimon Peres calls for a Palestinian state.

1998

23 October   Israel and the PLO sign the Wye River Memorandum under U.S. auspices.

1999

7 February   King Hussein of Jordan dies.

12 May   Ehud Barak is elected prime minister of Israel.

4 September   Israel and the PLO sign the Sharm el-Sheikh Memorandum (also known as Wye II).

10 November   Israel opens one of the "safe passage routes" along existing roads that connect the West Bank and Gaza

2000

11 July   Israeli-Palestinian negotiations at Camp David begin.

28 September   Israeli leader Ariel Sharon visits the Haram el-Sharif in Jerusalem, setting off the worst violent clashes (known as the Al-Aqsa *Intifada*) in Israel and the Occupied Territories since Israel was founded.

2001

6 February   Sharon is elected Prime Minister of Israel. Sharon's right-wing government begins the escalation of confrontations with the Palestinian Authority and Hamas in the Gaza Strip.

The rest of the year witnesses significant intensification of Israeli attacks on Palestinian Authority institutions, some in retaliation to Palestinian acts of resistance and suicide bombings but also in an apparent sustained campaign to weaken and undermine the Palestinian Authority and the prospects of emergence of an independent State of Palestine.

The attacks and counterattacks and suicide bombings caused the deaths of hundreds of innocent individuals.

2002

January   Israeli occupation forces begin withdrawal from areas that had been under civilian Palestinian administration in accordance with the Oslo Accords. This is because the United States dispatched General Anthony Zinni (Ret.) as special envoy to mediate between the parties and restart peace negotiations. The mission fails.

March–April   In an extensive and destructive approach, Israeli occupation forces reinvade and reoccupy Palestinian urban centers that are under the civil administration of the Palestinian Authority. The attack on the city and Refugee Camp of Jenin is especially bloody.

Israeli military systematically destroys Palestinian physical and institutional infrastructure. Headquarters of Palestinian president Yasser 'Arafat are severely damaged. His compound is surrounded by armored Israeli troops and he is effectively isolated and imprisoned in a couple of rooms there. The Palestinian Authority institutions and most functioning non-governmental institutions are effectively destroyed. Services to the Palestinian civilian population is halted, and even schooling is severely disrupted.

The Church of the Nativity is besieged by Israeli troops as Palestinian resistance fighters take refuge there.

Israel institutes an oppressive siege of Palestinian towns and cities. Movement of Palestinians for work, shopping, school and university and medical treatment is harshly curtailed. Humanitarian crisis looms.

15 March   The United Nations Security Council passes a U.S.-sponsored resolution calling for Palestinian statehood and calling on both parties in the conflict to honor an immediate cease fire in the 16–17 month warfare. Attacks by Israel escalate and many more civilians are killed.

4 April	Israeli helicopter gunships attack Palestinian activists near the Church of the Nativity, killing a 65-year-old Italian priest and injuring a number of nuns.
9 April	Israeli Foreign Minister Shimon Peres admits that the Israeli occupation forces carried out a large scale massacre of Palestinian civilians in Jenin.
9 May	Negotiators announce a breakthrough to end the five-week siege of the Church of the Nativity by Israeli troops.
23 July	The Israeli movement "There Is a Limit," which advocates rejection of military service in the Occupied Palestinian Territories, declares that 140 Israeli soldiers were imprisoned for refusal to serve in the occupation forces.
5 September	Israeli government rejects a European Union peace proposal presented by the Danish foreign minister to Israel and the Palestinian Authority.
16 October	B'Tselem, an Israeli Human Rights group, issues a report on Israeli occupation practices titled "Letha Curfew," describing the siege and curfew imposed by Israeli troops on Palestinian villages, towns, and cities as a "sweeping means to collective punishment."
2003	New U.S. "peace" proposals, especially the Road Map, go nowhere. Palestinians accept it, but Israelis indicate 14 objections. Siege and assassinations of Palestinian activists by Israel and Palestinian suicide bombings continue.

Palestinian Authority is paralyzed and unable to function to provide services to Palestinian civilians in the context of the continuing siege and curfew imposed on Palestinian population centers. Escalation of assassination by Israeli military (labeled as "targeted killings" by Israel) of Palestinian activists and resistance leaders.

The Peace Process and the Road Map are at an impasse. No progress on negotiations or relief of Palestinian population centers takes place. European states and the United Nations criticize Israel for the human rights violations in the occupied territories. They also criticize Palestinian suicide bombings. The Israeli occupation, siege, and curfew in Palestinian centers continue, and a humanitarian dilemma bordering on the crisis is in full swing. UNRWA launches a drive to help Palestinian civilians in the Gaza Strip. Unemployment rates among

Palestinians reach 60 percent in the Gaza Strip and between 40 and 50 percent in the West Bank.

The Bush administration supports the government of Prime Minister Ariel Sharon; President Bush calls Sharon a "man of peace," spurring international outrage. This adds to a negative view of the Bush administration not only among the Palestinians but among Arab and Muslim populations throughout the world.

2004

22 March   Israel assassinates Sheik Ahmad Yassin, founder and spiritual leader of Hamas.

1

Context and History

The land and people of the area historically called Palestine are ancient and have been at the center of regional and global history for millennia. They continue to be so today. Analysts in the West and in the Middle East believe that the Palestine question, at the heart of which is the Palestinian people, is the central issue in war and peace in the region. The contemporary conflict between Palestinians and Israelis revolves around Israeli occupation of the Palestinian territories of the West Bank and the Gaza Strip. As dramatic and newsworthy the occupation and resistance to it is, it is only half the problem of the conflict. What typically remain unstated, unreported, and uninvestigated in the Western media are the rights (particularly the right of return to their homeland, that is, the repatriation) of the Palestinian refugees who comprise more than half the total population of Palestinians in the world. Resistance to the occupation that has been in place for 37 years has ebbed and flowed over the years, but it has never ceased nor has that of the Palestinian refugees. They both continue to this day and are the core political problem in the Middle East.

This chapter establishes the contextual basis that will help the reader understand Palestinian history, society, and culture. It will combine a chronological historical rendition with fundamental concepts that will organize and make sense of the complex social, cultural, and political history of Palestine and the Palestinian people. These elements include Palestine's role in the greater regional Arab context, the Palestinian people's place in the larger Arab nation, its long-standing political struggle, the sociocultural dimensions and experiences that make up the unique Palestinian identity, the Palestinians' view of that identity, and the views of others about them.

THE LAND

Historic Palestine, the homeland of the Palestinians, is a small country the size of Vermont, about 10,435 square miles. It is situated in the southern half of the land in the eastern Mediterranean Sea. It is bounded in the east by the north-south line of the Jordan River, which flows from Lake Tiberius (also known as the Sea of Galilee) at its northern end and into the Dead Sea at its southern end. South of the Dead Sea is the dry Wadi Araba valley, which represents the border between historic Palestine and Jordan. Palestine's western border is the Mediterranean Sea. East of this north-south Lake Tiberius–Jordan River–Dead Sea and Wadi Araba boundary is the modern country of Jordan, on the northwest is Syria, on the southwest is the Sinai desert of Egypt, and on the north is Lebanon. The Jordan River is shallow and cannot be used for navigation. It is important, however, for irrigation.

Although a small country, Palestine is complex geographically and divided into five distinct zones. The first is the coastal plain along the Mediterranean, which is quite fertile in the north but less so in the south. It is, however, bisected in the north at the city of Haifa by Mount Carmel. The second zone, the spine of the country, includes the hills of a mountain range that also runs north-south. In the south, these hills begin with Jabal al-Khalil or Mount Hebron, moving north to Jabal al-Quds or Mount Jerusalem, then Jabal Nablus or Mount Nablus (the Samarian hills), and finally ending with al-Jaleel, the Galilee hills in the north. Some of these hills reach a height of about 3,000 feet above sea level. These hills are largely rocky but have been extensively terraced by the indigenous Palestinians over the past several centuries. The hill country is fairly dry and planted widely with olive trees, as well as, to a lesser extent, almonds, apples, and other fruit trees. Sesame also grows in these hills, whereas the flat plains and terraces that exist in the hill country are typically planted with wheat, barley, and lentils. The plains, valleys, and hills, especially with their terraces and their traditional limestone houses, are picturesque, evoking biblical pastoral and village images.

The Galilean hills north of Samaria are bisected by a triangular valley-plain, called Marj Ibn 'Amer, that runs from the northwest toward the southeast, the third distinct geographic zone, a very fertile area that separates to some degree the Palestinian mountain range. Traditionally it was planted with grains and legumes. East of the hill country is the Jordan valley rift and the Ghawr, the fourth distinct zone of historic Palestine. This area, below sea level and north of the Dead Sea, is blessed with fertile soil but few water resources. The Ghawr valley reaches 1,296 feet below sea level, the lowest point on earth. Even in the winter, the climate there is that of a vast natural hothouse. Accordingly, with irrigation from the Jordan River and wells, this region produces summer vegetables, including tomatoes, even in the winter months.

The fifth distinct zone is the desert area of al-Naqab in the south, a region that comprises nearly half the country. The al-Naqab desert is shaped as an inverted triangle. At the narrow southern end or apex is the seaport town on the Gulf of

Aqaba. To the north, the desert plain extends from the border of Egypt to the border of Jordan. The desert plain is largely infertile, but some grain does grow in its northern reaches in the center of which is the northern city of Bir Es-Sabe' (renamed "Beersheba" in modern Israel).

Historic Palestine had long been an administrative entity during the Ottoman period and became modern Palestine under the League of Nations Mandate in the wake of World War I. It was, however, dismembered in the course of the conflict that led to the creation of the state of Israel in 1948. The war in 1948, which involved Jewish military forces in Mandate Palestine and several Arab expeditionary forces ended in an armistice agreement between the warring parties. This agreement confirmed the geographic division of the country into the state of Israel, which occupied and gained control of a contiguous area of 78 percent of the country. The remaining 22 percent of the Palestinian territories in east-central Palestine (later known as the West Bank, because of its position on the Jordan River), was behind the military lines of the Jordanian armed forces facing the Israeli army and the Gaza Strip was behind the Egyptian military lines. These two regions are what are conventionally and contemporaneously known as Palestine or the Occupied Palestinian Territories.

These Palestinian territories were conquered and occupied by Israel in the 1967 Arab-Israeli war (generally called the Six Day War in Israel and the West). The ongoing dramatic conflict between the Palestinians and Israelis in historic Palestine is largely over Israel's occupation and colonization of the Palestinian territories of the West Bank and Gaza Strip. An agreement between Israel and the Palestine Liberation Organization (PLO), known as the Oslo Accords, was negotiated in Oslo, Norway, and signed on the lawn of the White House, dividing the occupied territories into three zones and allowing the Palestinian leadership of the PLO to establish the Palestinian Authority (PA), with responsibility only for civil affairs in the major cities of the West Bank and the Gaza Strip. The second zone established a shared Israeli-Palestinian authority, and the rest of the area, the third zone, remained under Israeli occupation. This agreement was supposed to be an interim measure for five years, leading to final negotiations that would establish an independent Palestinian state in the West Bank and the Gaza Strip and resolution of other outstanding issues. This plan was never implemented, however, a fact that, together with the continuing occupation, is the current source of conflict and the low-intensity warfare in the area.

The Climate

The climate of both historic Palestine and the contemporary Palestinian territories is mild Mediterranean weather, not unlike that of Greece and southern Italy and somewhat like that of southern California. The weather is hot and dry during the summer and cool and wet during the winter months. Rain falls principally in the winter and to a lesser extent in spring, whereas the summer months (and much of the fall) are dry. Occasionally in the winter, snow falls on the country's higher hills. The summer can be quite warm but not unpleasant; it is relatively humid along the coast and drier inland. Accordingly, much of the traditional agriculture, especially in the hill areas (where olive trees, almond trees, sesame bushes, grains, and legumes grow), and the natural flora of the country survive on relatively little rain in the winter and spring seasons. In the coastal plains, rainfall and irrigation made it possible to establish citrus orchards, a popular export since the nineteenth century.

The People

The Palestinians are the indigenous people of historic Palestine. They are culturally Arab and largely but not wholly Muslim. Many Palestinians are Christian Arabs who also have a very long heritage in Palestine and the rest of the region. The language of the Palestinians is Arabic, and they share their language and culture with the rest of the Arab world, of which they have been a part for centuries. Palestinians are descendents of an extensive mixing of local and regional peoples, including the Canaanites, Philistines, Hebrews, Samaritans, Hellenic Greeks, Romans, Nabatean Arabs, tribal nomadic Arabs, some Europeans from the Crusades, some Turks, and other minorities; after the Islamic conquests of the seventh century, however, they became overwhelmingly Arab. Thus, this mixed-stock of people has developed an Arab-Islamic culture for at least fourteen centuries, since the rise of Arab Islam in A.D. 610. Indeed, Palestine became the land bridge between Arab Muslim Asia and Arab Muslim Egypt and North Africa.

This Arab identity became all the more significant since 1948 when Palestine was dismembered and its people divided and dispersed throughout the region and the world. In the course of the 1948 war that dismembered Palestine geographically and established the state of Israel, the Palestinian people became divided into three numerically unequal and widely dispersed population segments. The first, comprising between 150,000–180,000 Palestinians, remained in their homes and on their land in what emerged as the state of Israel in 1948; overnight they found themselves strangers in their own country, a minority in a Jewish state. The second segment, comprising 500,000 Palestinians, remained in what became the West Bank and the Gaza Strip, behind Arab military lines. The third segment, comprising more than 750,000 of an estimated population of 900,000 in the areas that came under Israeli control, became refugees, expelled by Jewish forces or fleeing the areas of conflict into the remaining Arab areas of Palestine or into the neighboring Arab countries of Lebanon, Syria, Jordan, and Egypt. In total, the Palestinian population in 1948 worldwide numbered an estimated 1.4 to 1.5 million. Of that, a little more than half became refugees and are now the largest contemporary segment of the Palestinian people. Table 1.1 shows estimates of the global distribution of the Palestinian people up to the year 2002.

Table 1.1
Estimated Palestinian Population in the World, End of 2002

Country	Percent	Number
In historic Palestine, Total	49.4	4,595,750
Palestinian Territories	38.2	3,559,998
Israel	11.2	1,037,752
In diaspora	50.6	4,709,471
Jordan	29.2	2,716,188
Lebanon	4.3	402,977
Syria	4.6	423,453
Egypt	0.6	60,114
Saudi Arabia	3.2	300,565
Kuwait	0.4	38,254
Other Gulf States	1.3	120,612
Iraq and Libya	1.2	112,177
Other Arab countries	0.1	6,333
North America	2.5	231,723
Other countries	3.2	295,075
Totals	**100**	**9,305,221**

Source: PCBS, Table, p. 1. Accessed at http://www.pcbs.org.

PALESTINE IN HISTORY

Palestine occupied a small area, and the Palestinians—the indigenous people of Palestine—are a small population, numbering a little more than nine million people in 2003. The territory, which acquired the name "Palestine" over the last two millennia since the Roman Empire, has had a long, complex, and eventful history. Part of the ancient Fertile Crescent in which the civilizations of antiquity emerged and at the crossroads of conquering armies and empires in ancient, medieval, and modern eras, it is also sacred to the three monotheistic religions of the Near East: Judaism, Christianity, and Islam. It is known to and considered by all three faiths as the Holy Land.

Palestine shares its history with the rest of the surrounding region. Long before the Christian era, it was the gateway to Egypt and the Fertile Crescent, and thus it was often incorporated into the ancient empires of Pharaonic Egypt, Babylonia, Assyria, Greek Hellenes, Rome, and Byzantium before the Muslim Arabs. Thus, from its pre-monotheistic era of being the land of the agrarian Canaanites and the trading and seafaring Philistines, Palestine came to be controlled by the Hebrew Israelite tribes until the Roman conquest in the first century before

Christ. With the emergence of Christianity under the Byzantine Empire that was centered in Constantinople (modern-day Istanbul in Turkey), Palestine and its people became largely Christian in religion and Byzantine Hellenic in culture and customs. Throughout these pre-Christian and Christian Byzantine eras, many varied peoples (some of whom are mentioned in the Bible) with different languages, cultures, customs, and tribal structures and traditions lived, traded, married, and occasionally fought each other for centuries. Although there were Arab tribes, several of whom were Christian, in and around the territory of Palestine, that also lived and traded with the varied peoples of the area, Palestine did not fully come under Arab influence until the Islamic conquests of the seventh century.

Islam, the third monotheistic faith to emerge in the Near East, began in A.D. 610 when, according to the Islamic tradition, the Prophet Mohammad received his first revelations from God, through the Archangel Gabriel. Mohammad built a small supratribal community or nation (*ummah* in Arabic) of Muslim faithful in the Arabian Peninsula. Under his second successor, the Caliph Omar, Jerusalem was conquered from the Byzantine Empire and Arab Muslims and Islamic rule came to Palestine. In A.D. 632, the Caliph Omar prayed in one corner of the high plateau inside the ancient city of Jerusalem, where shortly thereafter the *Al-Aqsa* Mosque was built. On the same plateau, the Omayyad Caliph Abdul-Malik (of the first major dynasty of the Arab-Islamic empire) built in A.D. 691 another mosque, the Dome of the Rock Mosque, that, with its beautiful and now-famous golden dome, has graced the skyline of Jerusalem ever since.

The Dome of the Rock Mosque is especially holy to Muslims because tradition holds that the Prophet Mohammad, during the night of *Al-Mi'raj,* miraculously ascended to and returned from heaven on a winged stallion (*Al-Buraq*) from the spot of that revered rock. Palestinians and all Muslims know the enclosure, which contains the two sacred mosques atop this Jerusalem plateau, as *Al-Haram Al-Sharif,* the Noble Sanctuary. Islamic tradition holds Palestine sacred. The *Qur'an,* the holy Islamic scriptures, refers to Palestine as the *al-Ard al-Muqaddasah,* the Holy Land, and the Arabic name for the city of Jerusalem, *Al-Quds,* simply means "The Holy."

Palestine is also no less holy to the indigenous Arab Christians who have long been an integral part of the Arab world. The status of Palestine as a Christian holy land was underscored by the presence in the country of central administrative religious institutions of three Arab Christian denominations. The Greek Orthodox (also known as the Eastern Orthodox or Arab Orthodox Church) Patriarchate of Jerusalem has jurisdiction over the three (Roman) districts of Palestine. So does the Latin (Roman Catholic) Patriarchate and the Anglican Bishopric of Jerusalem. Jerusalem is also an important seat for other eastern churches such as the Coptic (Egyptian) and Armenian.

Over the years since the seventh century, the population of Palestine had become fully Arabized and largely Islamized. From its inception, Islam has been, contrary to common Western perspectives of it, a very tolerant religion. The

Jerusalem steps. © E. Y. Farsakh

Prophet Mohammad recognized, praised, and valued the Jewish and Christian prophets, including Christ, who preceded him and called the Christians and Jews of the region the "People of the Book," the Bible or Holy Scriptures, who should be allowed under Muslim rule to practice their respective faiths and live by their own religious laws—subject, however, to the payment of a poll tax, a tax levied and collected by the respective religious leaders as payment for Muslim state protection. It was this policy that allowed the local and regional Christians and Jews to survive and even flourish under Islamic Arab rule.

Palestine, called Jund Filastin ("district of Palestine") by the Arab rulers of the region in early medieval times, was always recognized as special and unique throughout Arab, and later Ottoman, history. Palestine, like the rest of the region, had become over the centuries Arabized in language and Islamized in culture and religion. Yet a significant minority, nearly 20 percent of the population, remained Christian in the early twentieth century. Since then, the Christian ratio has declined as a result of differential birth rates. Thus, Palestinian Arabs—Christian and Muslim—lived in the territory of Palestine continuously for nearly 1,400 years, until 1948, when as a result of the establishment of the state of Israel, the majority of the Arab population of Palestine, both Christian and Muslim, became refugees outside their traditional homeland. How and why this happened are crucial to the history, identity, culture, and society of the modern Palestinians and is reviewed in a following section.

Following the emergence of Arab Islam in the seventh century, Palestinian history continued to be eventful. There were three significant developments during the middle part of the medieval period: the European Christian Crusades, the Mongol Invasion, and later the rise of the Ottoman Empire. The European Christians, encouraged by Popes and Christian European kings, launched a series of Crusades, beginning in the eleventh and ending in the thirteenth century, to liberate the Holy Land from Muslim rule. The Crusades were devastating to the lands they passed through but particularly to the region of the Near East. In Palestine, especially in Jerusalem, the Crusaders massacred the Arab Muslims and their Christian Arab allies, looting much of the region. Thus, the history of the Crusades in Palestine and its region was savage, bloody, and long. Crusaders established feudal Latin kingdoms along the long coast of the eastern Mediterranean for nearly two centuries. Since that period the term "crusade" has had very negative connotations in the Arab world.

The Crusades came to an end beginning in A.D. 1187 when the Muslim commander, Saladin (Salah Ed-Deen), defeated the combined European armies under the leadership of King Richard the Lion Heart of England in a major battle near the village of Hittin, Palestine. Arab and Islamic rule, language, culture, and society were reestablished in the country.

The second major historical development was the Mongol invasion, which devastated the region. The Mongols destroyed Baghdad, the seat of the second major dynasty of Islamic Arab rule (the Abbasid Dynasty), and in A.D. 1258 ended Arab rule over the region. The Mongol invasion destroyed the economy, institutions, and society of the time. It took the area a long time to recover from its depredations. Although the Mongols occupied Palestine briefly on their way to conquer Egypt, they were defeated in the battle of Ayn Jalout (Spring of Goliath) by a new rising Muslim Egyptian power, the Mamlukes. A slave dynasty, the unique Mamlukes controlled Palestine from the thirteenth century until A.D. 1517, when they were defeated by a new power to the north, the Turkish Ottomans.

Much of the Arab world, including the province of Palestine, and much of southeastern Europe came under Turkish Ottoman dominion by the sixteenth century. Ottoman rule in Palestine and the rest of the Arab world lasted for 400 years. Only in 1917, toward the end of World War I, were the Ottomans finally expelled from Palestine and the Arab region. The Ottomans were Muslim Turks, and although they ruled the territory of Palestine and the Arab provinces for such a long time, no process of Turkification took place. Accordingly, Palestine remained Arab Muslim, with a significant community of Arab Christians.

MODERN HISTORY

The modern history of Palestine begins around 1800 and ends in 1948, the year of Palestine's *al-Nakba*, the Arabic term for the catastrophic destruction of the country, that is, its geographic dismemberment and the dispossession, destitution, and disbursement of its people. This modern period is divided into two distinct eras: the first covers the Ottoman period of the nineteenth century up to World War I; the second is the era of the British Mandate of Palestine, established by the League of Nations in the post–World War I period, and includes the period between the world wars and up to 1948.

The formal action of creating the British Mandate of Palestine by the victorious European powers in the wake of World War I only confirmed the long modern process of direct European intervention in Palestine and the region, ever since the Napoleonic invasion of Egypt and Palestine in 1798–1801. European intervention since the early nineteenth century has significantly transformed the social, economic, and political history of the Middle East in general and of Palestine in particular. European intervention in Palestine not only transformed the economic and political structure of the country—for example, capitalizing the subsistence and feudal landholding economy, generated a market economy, created new social classes, and new lifestyles, norms and values, and rearranged

Shopkeeper. © E. Y. Farsakh

Selling grapes. © E. Y. Farsakh

power relations among the existing and new social groups; it also, and above all, encouraged a process of European, especially Jewish, colonial settlement in the country. This initiated a dramatic process of demographic transformation of the country's population. Significant as well in the process of European intervention was the establishment in Palestine of European trade, religious and educational institutions that included monasteries, hostels, and other establishments for Christian pilgrims and schools for the local Arab Christians. This process of European intervention started slowly and intensified throughout the late Ottoman era of the second half of the nineteenth century but picked up significant momentum during the British Mandate of Palestine (1920–48).

WORLD WAR I AND ITS AFTERMATH

In the war between the British Empire and Ottoman Turkey, the British agreed to support the creation of an independent Arab Kingdom of the leaders of the great Arab Revolt against the Ottomans. Simultaneously, and in violation of that agreement, the British also agreed with their French allies—in the Sykes-Picot

Treaty—to divide the Arab domains of the Ottoman Empire among themselves. Most pivotal for Palestine, however, was a third "deal" that the British made during the course of World War I. The British government made a declaration to the nascent Jewish Zionist political movement in England (and the rest of Europe) in support of the idea of creating a "homeland for the Jews in Palestine." Known as the Balfour Declaration—named after Sir Arthur Balfour, its author and then British Foreign Secretary—this declaration and the actions derived from it not only doomed Arab Palestine but also changed forever the social and political history of the country and the region.

The post–World War I period witnessed the creation of the League of Nations by the victorious allies. The victorious British and French allies accorded themselves, in accordance with the Sykes-Picot Treaty, control over the liberated Arab regions of the Ottoman Empire. In turn, they divided up those regions into the Mandate states of Syria, Lebanon, Palestine, Transjordan (later, in the 1950s, Jordan), and Iraq. Thus the British and French fragmented the Arab east into several small states. Of course, as noted in the Balfour Declaration, Palestine was singled out as the future homeland for the European Jews, and this provision was incorporated by the British into the League of Nations' Mandate of Palestine.

THE BRITISH MANDATE OF PALESTINE: THE ROAD TO AL-NAKBA

After a short military administration in the wake of World War I, the British Empire created the Government of Palestine in 1921 and began to implement the provisions of the Balfour Declaration. Palestine, like Syria and Lebanon, was classified as a Class A Mandate by the League of Nations. Yet although the British and the French established indigenous governments in the other Class A Mandates in the region, the British ruled Palestine directly. They rejected Palestinian Arab protests to this violation. Furthermore, although there was only a tiny Jewish minority in the country, as there was in Syria, Lebanon, Iraq, and Egypt, the British established Arabic, English, and Hebrew as official languages and equated the Jewish community, which was less than 10 percent of the population, to the Palestinian Arab community in political representation and power in the varied institutions of government. The British Government of Palestine also refused to establish a democratic legislative body (as they did elsewhere in the other Arab countries they created) to be elected popularly by the electorate. Instead, they attempted to create an appointed council of equal numbers for the tiny Jewish community and the overwhelming Palestinian Arab majority. This never came to fruition. As direct rulers of Palestine, the British authorities then set about in a systematic manner the implementation of the Balfour Declaration and the Zionist project in Palestine.

Implementation of the Zionist Project in Palestine

The Zionist project in Palestine went beyond the undefined British idea of a "homeland for the Jews." Zionist ideology and plans called for the creation in

Palestine of a Jewish state. Not just that but a "state that is as Jewish as England is English." This project involved four major aspects: (1) Jewish in-migration and demographic transformation of the country, (2) Jewish land acquisition, (3) a separate Jewish economy and separate social and political institutions, and (4) a Jewish state within a state in Arab Palestine. All this strategy was put in place because the nascent and expanding Jewish community in the country was privileged and protected by the British authorities to create, in the final analysis, a Jewish state in Palestine irrespective of the wishes of the indigenous Palestinian Arabs. The following sections briefly review these actions.

In-Migration of European Jews

Perhaps the most significant aspect of the Zionist strategy was migration and settlement of European Jews in the country. The British colonial government of Palestine opened the gates of immigration during the Mandate period. Although Jewish religious migration into Palestine began in 1882, Jews numbered no more than 10 percent of a population of more than 750,000 according to a British census in 1922. Although the Palestinian Arabs officially comprised 90 percent of the population, many demographers believe there may have been more of them than the census shows.

Most Jews in Palestine lived in the urban areas of west Jerusalem and in the Tel Aviv suburb of the coastal Palestinian city, Jaffa. Jewish migration into Palestine under the British Mandate consisted of three major waves in each of the decades of British control. In the 1920s, more than 100,000 immigrants entered the country. By the 1931 census, the ratio of Jewish settler-immigrants to indigenous Palestinians began to shift significantly. Of the 1.04 million people in Palestine, 16 percent were Jewish and 84 percent were Arab. Although the rise in the Palestinian population was largely due to natural increase, the increase in the Jewish population was largely the result of British sponsored in-migration. The second major wave during the Mandate period occurred between 1932 and 1938 when nearly 200,000 central and east European Jews migrated to British-controlled Palestine. Thus, the European Jewish population jumped to 28 percent in a very short time. As a result of the third major wave of immigration, during World War II and its immediate aftermath, Palestine's Jewish population ratio reached 31 percent, while the Arab population declined to 69 percent of a total of 1.9 million people in 1947. Still, only one year before Israel was declared a state, the Jewish population constituted a minority of less than one-third.

Land Acquisition

Zionist ideology always portrayed Palestine as a land without people for a people without a land. Despite this ideology, Palestine was a densely populated and an intensively cultivated country. The Zionist attempt to acquire land in Palestine went through two distinct stages. The first was an effort to purchase land from Palestinians by Zionist organizations set up specifically for that purpose. The Zionist policy of land acquisition had a political and strategic logic in terms of location within the country, size, and contiguity. To begin with, the Zionists pressured and received from British Palestine Mandate authorities tens of thousands of acres of state land. They also tried repeatedly to purchase large tracts of agricultural land from large Palestinian landowners. They succeeded in purchasing Palestinian land from large landowners who found themselves in the newly created country of Lebanon and had difficulty managing their properties in what became Palestine. By 1948, Jewish settlers and Zionist organizations had acquired by purchase no more than 7 percent of Palestinian land. In the course of the military conquest of the country, however, the newly founded Jewish state of Israel (1948) gained 78 percent of the land of Palestine, a country the size of Vermont. Thus, European Jewish settlers acquired most of historic Palestine by force, thus dispossessing most of the indigenous Palestinians, who became refugees.

A Separate Jewish State within a State

Jewish separatism in Palestine started from the first decade of the British Mandate over the country, and the Jewish community was privileged, empowered, and protected by the British colonial authorities. The British facilitated the building of an exclusive Jewish economy by providing the Jewish community with major economic monopolies, allowing Jewish-owned economic enterprises to hire only Jewish labor, and paying higher wages to Jewish labor in government economic activity than their Palestinian counterparts received. The British also allowed and protected separate Jewish labor unions, educational institutions, and political organizations. In so doing, the British permitted and protected the Jewish minority community as a built a tightly organized "state within a state." This was fortified by the British authorities' recruitment of immigrant Jews to fight the Palestinian rebellion against British rule, which raged between 1936 and 1939, and their subsequently allowing Jewish settlers to develop armed groups within the country before, during, and after World War II. Thus, when the conflict between the Palestinians and the Jewish community and British authorities intensified after World War II, the Jewish community was well situated politically, economically, and militarily to win a war against the poorly organized indigenous Palestinians in 1947 and against the Arab expeditionary forces in the war of 1948.

The internal Palestinian conflict in 1940s intensified after Britain gave up its Mandate over Palestine and placed the problem before the newly founded United Nations. The United Nations voted in 1947 to partition Palestine into an Arab state and a Jewish state without consulting the Palestinian people. The partition plan was biased toward the proposed Jewish state in terms of land, and the areas were gerrymandered to create a state with a slight Jewish majority of 55 percent to 45 percent of Palestinians; the projected Palestinian Arab state would have had less land but a majority of nearly 95 percent Palestinians . The Palestinian Arabs naturally were unhappy about the partition of their country. The newly migrant Jewish community in Palestine found the results in its favor. Furthermore, as the conflict intensified, Jewish forces launched a systematic campaign to conquer more land and expel the Palestinian inhabitants. This was the origin of the Palestinian refugee problem of 1948. Equally important in the disaster that had befallen the Palestinian people was the fact that no Palestinian Arab state was founded as proposed by the United Nations. East-central Palestine remained behind Jordanian military lines and was annexed by Transjordan early in the 1950s to become the West Bank. The Gaza Strip, a Palestinian area that was behind Egyptian military lines, came to be administered by the Egyptian authorities.

AL-NAKBA AND ITS AFTERMATH

Al-Nakba is Arabic for "catastrophe" and is the word used by Palestinians to describe the traumatic experience of the destruction of their society in 1948 and the dispossession and expulsion of most of its people as stateless refugees. The Palestinian Nakba of 1948 dispossessed and dispersed the Palestinian population into the three major segments as identified earlier. Since that time, the social, economic, and political histories of the three communal segments proceeded along different trajectories influenced by the context of their existential situation in the host countries, in the territories of the West Bank and the Gaza Strip, and inside Israel for those who remained on their land and in their homes. Next, the destiny and contributions of each of the segments are reviewed.

The Palestinian Refugees and Their Diaspora Communities

What is significant about the destruction of Palestine as a country is the commensurate collapse of the Palestinian institutions and political organizations. Leaderless, politically disorganized and unable to return to their villages and towns in their homeland after the hostilities ceased, Palestinian refugees began to forge meager livelihoods in the areas and countries in which they sought refuge: the remaining areas of Palestine and the Arab host countries. In the initial phases the refugees relied on their extended families and kinsmen, a long-established tradition among Palestinians and other Arabs in the region, for economic support and security. Shortly after 1948, however, the United Nations erected dozens of refugee camps in the areas and countries of refuge for the least fortunate among them and created the United Nations Relief and Works Agency (UNRWA) to deliver to them humanitarian aid. By 1995, there still were 19 refugee camps in the West Bank, 8 in the Gaza Strip, 12 in Lebanon, and 10 each in Jordan and Syria. The locations of the camps were determined by the host countries and in the West Bank and Gaza Strip in accordance with local political and economic considerations.

In one generation, these camps developed from precarious wind-swept tent conglomerations with no infrastructure of services into highly congested shanty-towns of concrete, asphalt, and often open sewers. Palestinian refugee camps are densely populated, complex minicities with their own shops, marketplaces, manufacturing activities and service providers, educational institutions, health clinics, and even welfare agencies. Initially, the uprooting of the Palestinians from their homeland did not seem to cause real change in their political consciousness. By the 1960s, however, modern secular sociopolitical organizations (student, women's, and worker) evolved and began to change not only the nature of political ideology (pan-Arab nationalist) and activism but also the traditional value system. Secular nationalist symbols, literature, songs, rallies, celebrations, and funerals for fighters who died in the course of the struggle against Israel proliferated. Their camp-based, segregated existence enabled the exiled Palestinians to maintain much of their pre-diaspora social and cultural distinctiveness—Arabic dialect, customs, dress, and folklore.

The experience of dispossession, expulsion from one's own country, being born in the diaspora—stateless, without rights and with a stigmatized identity—is common to all Palestinians. For the majority, life was always insecure and existence precarious. Life in the camps remained difficult, unhealthy, overly congested, and brutish. By the mid-1990s many Palestinians sought residence outside the congested and unhealthy camps. Camp dwellers have come to comprise 55 percent of UN registered refugees in Gaza, 52.2 percent in Lebanon, and 22.8 percent in Jordan. Most middle-class Palestinians, however, preferred and were able to live outside the UN refugee camps. These latter groups established their own independent residences in what emerged as neighborhoods in cities in the Arab countries where they took refuge.

Over the nearly three generations since al-Nakba, voluntary migration in search of a better and more independent livelihood took Palestinian refugees to the Arab oil-exporting countries of the Gulf with their booming economies and to Europe and the Americas. The pattern of distribution by the beginning of the third millennium is indicated in Table 1.1. Most Palestinians are in the diaspora. The Palestinian communities have become differentially integrated economically and socially in varied host countries. Economic integration, social structure, and political conditions of the Palestinian communities varied significantly in their Arab host countries. Determinants of the host country's treatment and attitude toward the Palestinian refugee community in their midst include size, the degree of its political influence and organization, and the degree of its economic role and integration. Where the size of the Palestinian community is large relative to the indigenous population, politically well organized (and especially if it is armed), and perceived as a political threat by the local elites, host states have attempted to suppress and control the Palestinians. Indeed, such efforts have led to military conflict and a type of civil and communal warfare. This was the case in Jordan in the late 1960s and early 1970s and in Lebanon in the 1970s and the 1980s. In short, the different Palestinian refugee communities have had differing social, economic, and political histories since 1948. Yet despite this, or perhaps because of it, their Palestinian identity and sense of common destiny have been reinforced.

Although stateless (except for Jordan, which granted them the right of citizenship, especially to the middle class and the native residents of the West Bank), Palestinian refugees have built vibrant and dynamic communities. They have also established new political organizations to preserve and enhance their iden-tity, their economic well-being, their social and cultural life, and their political rights and aspirations. Palestinians in the diaspora have transformed themselves from what they were prior to 1948—a nation of largely illiterate peasants, farm-ers, and traditional rural residents—into varied and dispersed communities of urban, literate, working-class, professional, and entrepreneurial people.

Remarkably, the small pre-al-Nakba middle class in pre-1948 Palestine flour-ished and expanded dramatically in exile. This social class rode the crest of the post–World War II economic growth and then oil-based economic boom in the region since 1973. Many achieved high social, professional, economic, and even political status in varied Arab countries. Perhaps even more achieved renown in academia, medicine, science, mathematics, engineering, journalism, and busi-ness, not only in the Arab World but also in Europe and the Americas. The growth and increased influence of the Palestinian middle class and entrepreneurs not only rode the crest of the economic boom of the region but also the tide of anticolonial and antiimperial pan-Arab nationalism, the ideology of which included the liberation of Palestine as a central tenet. As a result, Palestinian social and physical mobility in the Arab region extended their political influence throughout the Arab World. This economic and political tide ebbed by the 1980s, however, and with this ebb came a contraction within the Arab world of Palestinian influence and the Palestinian cause.

The Palestine Liberation Organization

In the immediate wake of the 1948 Nakba, the dispossessed and traumatized Palestinians spontaneously articulated a simple hope: *Innana 'Ai'doun*—"we shall return." This slogan among the refugees developed into a mystique of redemption and return to their homes and homeland, and the sentiment quickly turned into political agitation. It is from among the Palestinian refugees that the earliest political organizations for regaining their human and political rights began. So, too, it is from among the newly expanded, flourishing and influential diaspora middle class that the leadership of the Palestinian political movements emerged. In response to such strong popular sentiment and escalating agitation, the League of Arab States (a regional organization similar to the United Nations) estab-lished in 1964 the Palestine Liberation Organization (PLO) to give formal voice, recognition, and structure to the pursuit of regaining Palestinian rights. The pan-Arab nationalist states of the period (especially Egypt, Syria, and Iraq) and many political parties and movements throughout the region promoted an ideology of liberation from foreign control as they struggled against the last vestiges of Euro-pean colonialism and the emergent interventionism of the United States and the Soviet Union of the post–World War II era. These states thus called for non-alignment in regard to Soviet-American rivalry and the Cold War.

The turning point for the PLO occurred in 1968. In the wake of the Arab states' defeat in the June 1967 Arab-Israeli war the old PLO reemerged radical-ized and revolutionary. The PLO was a creature of the times, influenced during the Cold War more by the Third World ideology of liberation than nonalignment. Its ideology and practice sought to transform the downtrodden Palestinian refugees from peasants into modern revolutionaries as the means to reclaim their rights and, in the course of that transform, their society as well. The ideology, goals, and strategy of the PLO evolved in four major phases that also had a direct bearing on its organizational evolution as well.

The first phase, between 1964 and 1968, was a start-up period during which the PLO was an organization created by the Arab League to contain Palestinian activism but also to give the Palestinians one voice. The second phase, between 1968 and 1982, was a period of revolutionary political development and expansion. During this period, the PLO established and expanded its civil service institutions, gave ideological specificity and coherence to the Palestinian political cause, transformed its political goals, made most of its political achievements, and placed the Palestinian question on the international diplomatic and political scene. Although this phase ended in military defeat as a result of the Israeli invasion of Lebanon and the exodus of the PLO fighters and bureaucracy from the city of Beirut in 1982, it nevertheless was the high-water mark for the diaspora Palestinians. It was during this period that the diaspora's political, social, and economic institutions were created and expanded. Among those that appeared were the Palestine National Council (PNC), which is the legislature in exile; the Central Council (a legislative-consultative subgroup of the PNC); the Political Department, or foreign diplomatic agency, and the Military Department; the Palestine Liberation Army, which comprised three brigades that were small in number and poorly equipped under the command of the host Arab states' military.

The new PLO also established the Palestine National Fund (a treasury); the Department of Education; the Red Crescent Society for health services; a social affairs institute; the Departments of Information, Popular Mobilization, and the Homeland; the Research and Planning Center; and Samed, its economic and investment arm. During this period, the PLO grew organizationally to provide needed services, protection, and leadership directly to diaspora Palestinians and indirectly for those in the West Bank and Gaza who had come under Israeli occupation in 1967. The PLO structure of the time was essentially a de facto government in exile.

Perhaps most significant during this period, the ideology and goals of the PLO were transformed and became more acceptable internationally. Beginning in a revolutionary flush, the PLO and its constituent political groupings formulated their goal (spelled out in its charter) as the liberation of all of Palestine from Zionist Jewish control and the return of the refugees to their homeland. It also spelled out the strategy as that of armed struggle and possibly a people's war of liberation. Its vision was of the creation of a secular democratic state for all peoples of Palestine—Muslim, Christian, and Jewish. This may have been both idealistic and unrealistic in the international context of the time. Thus, it received no international resonance. As the international and regional political context changed significantly, Arab states were accommodating each other and Western powers. By 1974, the PLO reformulated its goal as a Palestinian state in the Occupied Territories of the West Bank and the Gaza Strip next to Israel to be achieved by diplomatic means. This famous "two-state solution" to the Palestinian-Israeli conflict has remained its goal until now. The PLO gained recognition for itself as the sole legitimate representative of the Palestinian people and was admitted into the United Nations with a permanent observer status. It was also during this period that the UN General Assembly passed a series of resolutions, including Resolution 2535, which recognized and affirmed the "inalienable rights of the Palestinian people."

The third phase began in 1982 and ended in 1993 when the Oslo Accords were signed between the PLO and Israel. This period was quite eventful internationally and included the collapse of Communism and the Soviet Union, the long Iraq-Iran war, and the Gulf War against Iraq (1991). The PLO blundered politically and became financially and diplomatically marginalized. As a result, many if not most of its institutions were financially squeezed and became ineffective in delivering the needed services to the Palestinian refugee communities in exile. Nor was it able to extend much support or guidance to the Palestinian people under occupation in the West Bank and the Gaza Strip. This was important, because conditions of Palestinian life under Israeli occupation became progressively and significantly worse. Indeed, because of the severe repression and exploitation, the Palestinians exploded into an uprising (an Intifada) in 1987 that lasted until 1993. The achievements accomplished by the PLO and the Palestinian people during the second phase seemed to unravel in the third phase, only to be dramatically reversed with the signing of the Oslo Accords that catapulted the PLO internationally into center stage once again.

The fourth phase began in 1993 and is ongoing. It has been characterized by dramatic political-diplomatic change in the PLO, the Palestine question, and the Palestinian people. The Oslo Accords focused attention on the Occupied Territories and on the politically marginalized diaspora communities that have been the anchor and driving force of the Palestinian political movement to regain the inalienable Palestinian rights. The agreements, supported by the United States and the international community, allowed the repatriation of the PLO leadership and bankrupt bureaucracy to the West Bank and the Gaza Strip. In accordance with the agreements, PLO leadership organized a civil authority (the Palestinian Authority [PA], or the Palestinian National Authority [PNA], as its Palestinian leadership prefers to call it).

The Occupied Territories were divided into three segments: the PA established civil authority over segment A, which comprised Gaza City, two-thirds of the Gaza Strip, and seven major cities in the West Bank. Segment B comprised many other smaller towns and villages in the West Bank, which became subject to joint Palestinian-Israeli control. Finally, segment C remained completely under Israeli control. This arrangement was to last for five years, when the final status of the Occupied Territories and other issues (refugees including compensation, Jerusalem, Israeli settlements, borders, etc.) were to have been decided.

The Occupied Territories of the West Bank and the Gaza Strip

The second segment of the Palestinian people has had a different but equally traumatic experience from that of the refugees. The 1948 war that established the state of Israel left two small areas of Palestine in Arab hands: east-central Palestine, behind Jordanian military lines, and the Gaza Strip, behind Egyptian military lines. The indigenous Palestinian residents of those two regions were joined in 1948 by Palestinian refugees expelled from the area of Palestine that became the state of Israel. Egypt administered the Gaza Strip as a separate territory, the destiny of which was to be determined when the Palestine question was resolved. In 1951, however, Transjordan formally annexed east-central Palestine and declared the new country the Kingdom of Jordan, comprising Transjordan (the east bank of the Jordan River) and east-central Palestine (the west bank of the Jordan River). The label "West Bank" became popularized as east-central Palestine ever since. Although only two countries recognized the annexation (Britain and Pakistan), the West Bank became de facto a part of Jordan. The Palestinians of the West Bank were also granted Jordanian citizenship.

In the Arab-Israeli war of June 1967, Israel conquered and occupied both territories of the West Bank and the Gaza Strip. These Palestinian territories have been under occupation ever since. Many peace initiatives were made in the wake of that war, starting with that of U.S. Secretary of State William Rogers in 1971 and including the Saudi Arabian initiative of Prince Abdullah in 2002 and the "Road Map" of the George W. Bush Administration. They all came to naught because Israel refused to withdraw completely from the Occupied Territories in return for peace with the Palestinians and the Arab World. To the contrary, shortly after the occupation of the Palestinian territories, Israel began to confiscate—illegally, according to international law—Palestinian land under its control and illegally establish Israeli Jewish colonial settlements. International law prohibits an occupying power to move its population into the occupied territory, and the UN charter to which Israel is signatory also prohibits the acquisition of territory by force.

After 1967, the Palestinians resisted in varied ways, but as the confiscation of land escalated and the occupation became more severe, those living in the occupied territories erupted into an Intifada of civil disobedience that lasted from 1987 until 1993. Palestinian youth and some young children threw stones at the Israeli tanks, armored personnel carriers, and troops only to be shot and frequently killed by the Israeli soldiers. The harsh practices on the part of the Israeli occupation army to suppress the Intifada caught the attention of world press and brought more attention to the Palestinian issue than ever before. The forgotten occupation suddenly exploded on the world scene, and placed the Palestinian question, especially the occupation of the West Bank and Gaza Strip, center stage on international political and diplomatic agendas. Television reports showed Israel in a new light as a bully beating up its Palestinian victims, reversing the long-standing Western image of Israel. Increasingly, the Palestinians of the West Bank and the Gaza Strip were portrayed as the little David confronting the Israeli Goliath.

The Intifada came to an end in 1993 as the Oslo Accords were signed and the Palestinian leadership established the Palestinian Authority and called on the Palestinians to end the uprising. With the return of the Palestinian leadership to the West Bank and Gaza Strip, the people's hopes soared in expectation of an end to Israeli occupation, land confiscation, and repression within the five-year period as specified in the Accords.

Developments since the 1993 agreement belied this hope. During the period of the Oslo peace process (1993–2001), Israel's policies in the Occupied Territories produced worsening conditions. Israel confiscated more land, established or enlarged more colonial settlements, and literally doubled the number of settlers. The number of Israeli settlers in the Occupied Territories increased to nearly 500,000 while the Palestinian population rose to nearly 2.5 million. During the Oslo period, Israel's per capita income soared from $12,600 to more than $20,000 and ushered in an era of unprecedented prosperity, while the Palestinian economy collapsed, triggering a decline of more than 25 percent in per capita income, skyrocketing rates of unemployment, and high rates of poverty, according to United Nations and World Bank reports. The Palestinian economy was subjugated by and heavily dependent on Israel. Some of the physical and social infrastructure also deteriorated, even though the international community provided economic aid to the Palestinian Authority.

In the end, it was the collapse of the political negotiations between Israel and the PA in the context of these worsening conditions and increasing Israeli provocations that led to the explosion of the second Intifada. The 2001 Intifada emerged more violent and bloodier than the first. Israel's response was to invade, reconquer and reoccupy the Palestinian cities, towns, villages, and refugee camps that had been given up to the civilian control of the Palestinian Authority through the Oslo agreements. The reconquest was so brutal, the killings so extensive and horrific, and the humanitarian crisis so deep that it created an international outcry.

In 2004, the right-wing government of Israel began to build a separation wall 30 feet tall (in some parts, it is a high, electrified wire fence) on occupied Palestinian land all along the Israeli border with the West Bank and around the Palestinian city of East Jerusalem, which includes the old city. The "Wall" snakes through the border areas, engulfing on the side of Israel large tracts of fertile agricultural land that belongs to Palestinian farmers and villagers, surrounding, economically strangling, and isolating Palestinian towns such as Qalqilia and cutting off Arab Jerusalem from the rest of the Palestinian territories. International critics of the separation wall have described it as an apartheid structure. The United Nations General Assembly asked the International Court of Justice (ICJ) at the Hague, the Netherlands, for a ruling.

After long deliberations, the ICJ issued its ruling describing the Wall as a violation of international law and the Fourth Geneva Convention. It recommended to the United Nations and Israel that the Wall should be dismantled and the land returned to its Palestinian owners. The General Assembly of the United Nations voted overwhelmingly in favor of a resolution in support of the ICJ ruling. Israel and the United States voted against the UN resolution. Israel ignored the recommendation and continued the erection of the illegal wall. The United States officially supported Israel's illegal position, as did the candidates in the 2004 U.S. presidential race. When completed, the Wall will divide the West Bank into disconnected and isolated Palestinian cantons and will, unless dismantled, destroy any prospect of establishing a contiguous independent Palestinian state. The separation wall has further increased the humanitarian crisis of the Palestinians. How and when this conflict will end depends largely on ending Israel's occupation of the West Bank and Gaza Strip.

The Palestinians in Israel

The third population segment of the Palestinian people, the smallest in number, remained in their homes and on their land after the establishment of the state of Israel in 1948. At the time, they numbered close to 180,000 people. Now they number more than 1.2 million. The Palestinians in Israel also tended to be concentrated in the northern part of the country, the Galilee hills, with the city of Nazareth having the largest population concentration.

The best characterization of the Palestinian segment that suddenly found itself in the state of Israel is a fictional portrayal by a Palestinian, novelist and politician Emile Habibi, who remained behind. The Palestinians in Israel were a community that has been part of an integrated Palestinian Arab society, an Arab majority in Palestine with its functioning institutions, lifestyle, and psychological and social makeup. Suddenly and incomprehensively, they found themselves a minority of an alien society imposed on them in their own homeland. Habibi captures this bizarre turn of events in a satirical short novel featuring a fictional character named Saeed, who became simultaneously a pessimist and an optimist about his situation. Habibi described this strange person as the "Pessoptimist." Although this character seemed to live in a Kafkaesque social and political environment in the new Israeli state, the Palestinian minority in Israel was immediately placed under a restrictive military rule until 1966. They were cut off from their Arab and Islamic environment in the region and treated inside Israel with suspicion as a Fifth Column, an internal population that is a threat to the security of the Israeli state. Only in 1967 when Israel conquered and occupied the West Bank and Gaza Strip did the Palestinian community in Israel come into contact with their Palestinian brethren and culture. From the start, the Palestinian community in Israel was subjected to a regime of internal colonialism. Over the years, this regime has been transformed, becoming more indirect and sophisticated, but its essence has remained in place.

Internal colonialism is a system characterized by four principal features: political control, economic exploitation, social segregation, and suppression of ideology, culture, and identity. To begin with, the Palestinians in Israel, who were primarily farmers, were systematically robbed of their land and over the years became the manual laborers and service workers of Israel. Their income levels are only a fraction of those enjoyed by Israeli Jews; they have poorer schools and lesser educational achievements. Indeed, they are the least educated of the three segments of the Palestinian population. As a result the quality of their life, measured in economic, housing, educational, health, and other measures, is far below that of their fellow Israeli citizens. Until recently, they were not allowed to form their own political parties or build institutions of higher education for themselves. Most relevant is the fact that the Israeli state, through the education system imposed on its Palestinian citizens and the control over their cultural activity, has attempted to suppress Palestinian Arab identity. Despite this, the Palestinian minority in Israel has grown in size and transformed socially and politically. It has often found cultural means, especially poetry, to express its Arab identity. The Palestinians in Israel are now a dynamic community with political importance and influence—not only in Israel, but also in Palestinian society in general.

2

Society and Social Customs

TRADITIONAL SOCIAL STRUCTURE

The Occupied Terriroties/Palestine is part of the Arab World. It shares with the rest of the Arab World, especially the countries that are its neighbors—Jordan, Lebanon, and Syria—a distinctive configuration of traditional and contemporary social structures, customs, values, and norms. These have been changing ever since the nineteenth century as a result of European intervention in what was then the Ottoman province of Palestine and the rest of the Arab "Fertile Crescent" region of the eastern Mediterranean Sea. Change has also come about because of the local and regional drive toward modernization that has been evolving ever since.

Prior to European intervention in Palestine, the province was largely based on an agrarian economy and a commensurate rural social system. It had a few small cities and towns that specialized in the production of certain products that were well known in the region. These included, among many, the famous soap, manufactured particularly in the city of Nablus; pottery and rugs in the city of Gaza; and glassware, pottery, and other products in the city of Hebron. Jerusalem, the center of administrative, religious and legal life, attracted religious pilgrims from the three major faiths: Islam, Christianity, and Judaism. Muslims and Arab Christians predominated as pilgrims. The indigenous Jews were a tiny minority in both Palestine and the adjacent Arab region. Jerusalem and its surrounding towns and villages such as Bethlehem, Beit Sahour, Beit Jala, and others also produced religious figurines and icons made of olive wood for the Christian pilgrims. Famous among them are the figures of the scene of the Nativity, including the infant Jesus, the Virgin Mary, the three Magi, and animals such as lambs, sheep, camels, and donkeys. In Nablus, Majdal, Ramallah, and other centers, cloth was woven on traditional handlooms and sold locally and, to some extent, around the region.

The most important economic activity of the great majority of the population was agriculture—both for subsistence and for the local and regional markets. The dry climate of the country allowed the planting and cultivation of olive trees in the hill country of central and northern Palestine. This tree has become a symbol of Palestine, both its past and its present. From olives, which were a main staple of daily food, came olive oil, a food staple that was also used for lighting and soap making. Even the olive pits were crushed and burned in special copper or earthen containers or braziers, for home heating in the cold winter months. When burned inside the house, olive pits produced little or no smoke and much heat. In addition to olive trees, the country's plains and flat plateaus were typically planted with wheat, and in the drier areas of the south, barley and other grains were grown. These products were produced largely for subsistence but also for the local and, to a lesser extent, regional, markets. Besides olives, the farmers and peasants of the hill country also produced sesame seeds and some cotton.

The nineteenth-century European intervention pushed Palestine increasingly into a market economy and linked it with Europe through export and import trade. The single most important product that Palestinians developed for export in the second half of the nineteenth century was citrus fruit, and oranges in particular. The coastal area was extensively planted with orange orchards and the fruit was exported to England and as far north as Moscow and St. Petersburg in Russia. Exported from the port city of Jaffa, the oranges came to be known as Jaffa oranges. Jaffa oranges became famous in large part because, before refrigeration, they were practically the only fruit available in northern Europe during the winter. They survived, sweet and juicy, the 23-day journey by ship from Jaffa to London and became very much valued at the time.

Palestinian farmers and landlords also exported sesame seeds to France, where they were ground into oil for use in the manufacture of perfumes. Hill wheat, called durum or hard wheat, was especially good for making spaghetti and other pastas, so it was imported extensively into Italy. Finally, one of the big exports of the nineteenth century was barley, sent to Germany to produce beer. Palestine in the nineteenth century also became a major tourist destination of Christian pilgrims from Europe and even America. In short, this economic transformation into a market economy that exported raw agricultural products had also a long-term negative socioeconomic impact on the country. This nineteenth-century pattern of exporting raw agricultural products, importing manufactured goods, and becoming a tourist attraction for Westerners are classic hallmarks leading to economic underdevelopment in the non-European world.

MODERNIZATION OF TRADITIONS

Social change in terms of economic activity, place of residence, social customs, values, and dress transformed Palestine further during the British Mandate period, between the two world wars. Such change then escalated dramatically as Palestine was dismembered and its people became refugees or succumbed to Israeli occupation in 1967.

Village and Folk Life

Until 1948, the year of al-Nakba, more than three-quarters of the Palestinians in Palestine lived in small villages. In the West Bank and Gaza Strip, the majority of the population still lives in villages and towns where the economy is based on agriculture. Village farmers and peasants derive their livelihood from the land and related economic activity. Whole families have traditionally worked the land together, and continue to do so today. Typically, villagers live in homes built from quarried stones (there are few forests and little lumber available for building) built side by side and go out to work in the fields that surround the village. Palestinian villages are composed largely of kinspeople. Indeed, villages may be described as communities of families organized in extended kin groupings—lineages or clans— called *hamayel* (in the plural; *hamula* in the singular). Some small villages have a single *hamula*, and other, larger ones may include two or more *hamayel*. A lifestyle characterized by communal cooperation, which existed in pre-1948 Palestine, continues to exist in the West Bank and Gaza Strip today, a pattern of residence and work that differs from farm life in the United States, where farmers typically live and work separately and independently on their own land.

Village social life is an intricate and complex set of interdependent relationships that combine social, economic, and political dimensions between the kin of a *hamula* and among the *hamayel* of the village or the district. In effect then, the basic social unit in the village is the extended family. Villages often are little more than conglomerations of extended families or groups of extended families, that is, *hamayel*. All village life is experienced and expressed through the extended family. Rural and agrarian Palestine is characterized by a residential family pattern in which households were typically clustered around the house of the patriarch. Palestinians in rural Palestine live in extended or near-extended household compounds in the villages and towns. Besides living together or nearby, rural extended families often work the fields and in other economic and social activities together and often consume their meals and spend leisure time together as well. During the long winter months when agricultural activity is minimal, the evenings are often spent in visits among family units. Often the men and women congregate separately. Evening entertainment may include the telling of folk or epic tales.

As land is central to their livelihood, the farmers' and peasants' relationship to the land is pivotal. Land is the source of livelihood and as such is the most cherished value in rural life. It also is the basis of the sense of belonging, of economic and psychological security, and of social and cultural continuity. Owning land thus allows the farmer a sense of security, belonging, honor, and pride of place. Lack of land ownership, as experienced among tenant farmers or sharecroppers, brings none of these. To lose land, a fact of life for Palestinians since al-Nakba in 1948 (continuing today via land confiscation for Israeli settlements, military bases, and roads), represents a sense of being uprooted, losing one's livelihood, insecurity, and defeat.

Land is a rich feature of rural life, in the villagers' collective memory and in their most deeply held values. Palestinians express their love of the land and its bounty in songs, poetry, and folktales that successive generations celebrate. Seasonal agricultural products such as oranges, almonds, pomegranates, grapes, figs, dates, and herbs (especially thyme) have special meaning for the villagers and are featured and honored during family, holiday, and life-cycle gatherings. Seasonal gifts from one family to another of fruits and herbs bring kin, neighbors, and friends closer together. Similarly, children often collect wild flowers that grow during the spring, such as the poppy, *anemone coronaria*, and cyclamens (called the Shepherd's Cane in Arabic) and present them as gifts. Poppies are especially abundant during spring, covering vast stretches of land and mountain slopes. Red or scarlet is the predominant color, but blue, purple, and white are also in plenitude. Given its extreme geographic variation, Palestine is a land of wild flowers that are dramatically different in variety and in color. Offering a sampling of this stunning variety is *The Wild Flowers of Palestine*, a beautifully illustrated book originally published in 1870 that has been reproduced by the Al-Qattan Foundation in London.

Since 1967, the pattern of earning a livelihood has changed significantly as two processes developed. The first is the Israeli occupation, which progressively forced a change in the labor structure for the Palestinian people. Out of necessity, more and more of them sought wage labor, considerably reducing their agricultural activity. High fertility rates and a rapid increase in the population have further accelerated this change. This, combined with the additional loss of land due to Israeli occupation, has left little that can sustain all those who wish to work it. A second factor is the regional development of the oil industry. The oil boom of the 1970s attracted many Palestinians to seek work in the oil-producing countries of the Arabian Gulf. Palestinian expatriate labor send home funds to their families, forging a greater reliance on wage labor and enhancing the development of a nonagrarian market economy. This move away from reliance on agriculture has had important consequences on the social organization and lifestyle of Palestinians in the West Bank and Gaza Strip.

Refugee Camp Life

In the wake of al-Nakba in 1948, the majority of the Palestinians suddenly became landless, urban residents in refugee camps near Arab cities. As refugees, the former farmers and peasant villagers sought jobs in service, construction, and manufacturing in metropolitan centers near their camps rather than in agriculture farther away. Now landless, they nonetheless retained and romanticized their love of the land and its bounty. "The land of Palestine and the lover become one and the same in the writings of the Palestinians Ghassan Kanafani and Mahmoud Darwish,"[1] two refugee authors who expressed in their own words the love for and loss of land that they and their compatriots felt. Kanafani titled a collection of short stories *The Sad Orange*, a selection for which he became famous. Darwish, the greatest Palestinian poet, and among the foremost contemporary Arab poets, introduced into his poetry rich, evocative imagery derived from the village and farming life of Palestine, using, for example, phrases and imagery such as "I call land the extension of my soul," "I am the land, plow my body," and "the land we carry in our blood." Darwish also includes imagery based on fruits of the land as in "the wedding of grapevines," and "I call birds, almonds and figs." He describes the Palestinian refugee as the "carrier of the agony of land."[2]

In many respects, the Palestinian refugees, although landless, have nevertheless reconstituted their family- and kin-based social groups, often including their extended families and *hamayel*, and continued to practice the customs and traditions that preserve the cherished values of village life. The kinship system in its smaller or larger groupings is their only social safety net, and has helped them survive, especially in the early years of exile. In their exile, they have continued to practice village customs and assert rural values, including gift giving when buying seasonal fruits in bulk and sharing their purchases. Thus, as reviewed later in the discussion of values, the refugees have not lost but in fact reproduced and reinforced their traditional values, norms, and customs.

City Life

With the growth of trade with Europe, Palestinian cities began to expand rapidly in the nineteenth century, and then even faster during the British Mandate period. Thus, as trade with Europe became an increasingly important economic activity in the nineteenth and twentieth centuries, more Palestinians moved into the coastal cities of Haifa, Jaffa, and Gaza, which were the pivotal links to trade. They also moved increasingly into Jerusalem, a city in the central hills, as the city grew in response to religious tourism. Of course the most important—and unexpected—event that abruptly and dramatically urbanized the largest proportion of the population was the mass expulsion and exodus of the Palestinians in 1948.

Urban Palestinian life before al-Nakba, and afterward in West Bank cities, Gaza City, and the urbanized camps near Arab metropolitan centers, differed somewhat from that in rural areas and villages. Urban Palestinians did not live in extended family compounds but in homes and apartments that were individual households for nuclear family units, with grandparents typically living in the household of their eldest son. One of the key changes that urbanization, modernization, and exile have brought has related to family life. Nonetheless, urban Palestinians maintain a close bond and extensive relations among their extended kin. Urbanization has ushered in a new family form among the Palestinians: the functionally extended family. Individual households that belong to the functionally extended family typically live separately and consume their meals separately but look out for each other and cooperate economically, socially, financially, and politically.

This type of family differs from the small, mobile American family in large part because the public and private institutions that serve the individual and the small family unit are absent for the Palestinians. For example, they cannot get a long-term mortgage to build or buy a home or get a bank loan to help pay for university. Thus, the individual and small family unit depend on the larger, functionally extended kinship group for such help. They share with kin when they can. It is a traditional value and an aspect of their survival strategy as stateless refugees.

Education: Refugees and Occupation

Through the education and training received at the United Nations Relief and Works Agency (UNRWA) in refugee camps, and independently in the West Bank and Gaza Strip, Palestinians after al-Nakba became a skilled and educated population. Many went on to higher education, becoming engineers, physicians, lawyers, businesspeople, bankers, accountants, auditors, teachers, professors, and other professionals. Quite a few have become prominent in their fields in the West Bank and Gaza, in the Arab World, and internationally. The Palestinians are the most highly educated population group per capita in the Arab World and the Middle East. Because of their skill levels and their willingness to move in search of secure positions, Palestinians have been migrating to find work since the 1950s, going especially to the oil-producing countries of the Arab Peninsula, the populations of which were and still are small and insufficiently skilled and which are in need of their services.

Indeed, the Palestinians became the most important expatriate Arab community that helped develop these Arab states through designing, building, and running the new governmental and social institutions and the physical infrastructure of those countries. By 1990, there was more than one million Palestinians living and working in the Arab oil-producing countries. In the wake of the Gulf War of 1991, however, Kuwait, accusing many Palestinians of collaborating with the Iraqi occupation, expelled most of its Palestinian residents (about 400,000), who then moved largely to Jordan but also to other places, including Europe and the Americas. It is estimated that there are about 150,000 Palestinians and Americans of Palestinian heritage in the United States. Even the Palestinian minority inside Israel has become more educated over the years and now has a professional class serving its community.

For Palestinians in exile, under occupation, or living inside Israel, education emerged as the most important value since al-Nakba—their only security in an insecure political and stateless world. Most adopted typical urban values of education and work. Both genders attend school and university, often in coeducational settings. Thus, the traditional values governing the separation of the sexes in public context have changed significantly in contemporary times, especially in

exilic Palestinian communities. For Palestinians, the pursuit of modern education actually conforms to their traditional value of hard work. They are fond of
expressing this value in proverbs that are commonly Arab, not just Palestinian,
such as, "Whoever toils will achieve," "The one who does not sow does not reap,"
and "hope without effort is a tree without fruit."

VALUES AND SOCIAL CUSTOMS

The financial difficulties in which most Palestinians found themselves after al-
Nakba together with changing labor markets led many women to seek paid
employment outside the home or the farm. This emerged as a new custom for
Palestinian women; traditionally women had worked in the home and the fields
alongside their family, *hamula*, and neighbors. It also led to some democratization
of relationship within the family, especially among the middle class.

Family is the foundation of social life in Palestinian society. Thus, support and
loyalty for family and kin are strong values. It became all the more so as the
majority of the Palestinians became refugees. Because there is no social security,
family and kin operate as a safety net. Such a function is the basis for the strong
bond among family members and the more extended kin. Associated with this
central social value is a set of other values, including generosity and hospitality.
Palestinians, like other Arabs, are a generous and hospitable people. Typically
they honor guests and family and kinship members, offering elaborate meals,
desserts, and Arabic or Turkish coffee. They spend much time eating, talking, and
gossiping about family members and relatives and village or neighborhood affairs.
They tell stories about the family, each other, and especially about the children;
they often tell traditional folktales as well. Such extended family gatherings
where so much hospitality is extended occur frequently, at least once or twice a
week and during holidays. Palestinians never seem to tire of them. Families are
typically large with several children ranging in number from 4 to 12. (Reportedly,
in recent surveys, most Palestinian women in the West Bank and Gaza Strip indicate that the ideal family size is between four and six children.) Indeed, these
gatherings are great festive occasions during which the large number of children
play, laugh, tease, and enjoy each other's company. The women typically prepare
the meals together, and the men congregate and discuss family affairs and politics.

Most traditional societies are typically patriarchal. Palestinian society is no
exception. Thus patriarchal relationships dominate social relations in the family,
at work, and often in public life. In this structure, the father, the patriarch, and
generally other men in the family assume responsibility for the well-being of the
family and wield relatively unchallenged authority. They expect obedience, loyalty, and respect from women and children. Kin cooperate to secure a livelihood,
gain a good living, and enhance the status of the family. Farms, businesses, and
other economic enterprises are often jointly owned. Families may pool resources
to send one of their own for higher or professional education. Thus, the success
or failure of an individual is the success or failure of the family as well. Patriarchal

values and relations typically predominate not only within the family but also in schools, the workplace, and religious and political organizations.

Nevertheless, the political, economic and social conditions of the Palestinian people in all three segments have forced some changes in this patriarchal system. The political and armed guerrilla movements that emerged in the wake of the June 1967 Arab-Israeli war introduced alternative organizational, associational, and work patterns. Some even proposed a revolutionary transformation of Palestinian society and social structure. Accordingly, these organized movements formed service and political organizations that were outside the kinship structure and more democratic and merit based. Thus, these new organizations emerged more modern in content and structure. An example is provided by the description of a Palestinian camp in the aftermath of the 1967 war.

After a three-week study of a Palestinian refugee camp in Jordan immediately after the June 1967 war, I concluded that a few well-armed men and well-organized persons might be able to invade and control this camp of more than three thousand people because the camp lacked organization. Every family lived on its own, totally preoccupied with immediate and personal problems and interests. Less than a year later, in the spring of 1968, I visited the same camp and found it totally transformed. In the meantime, Palestinian resistance organizations had mobilized the people, trained them, engaged in political dialogue, and involved them in preparation for surprise attacks.[3]

Since the rise of their contemporary liberation movement, Palestinians have increasingly adopted modern values, modern organizations, and modern social relations as they mobilize politically, migrate internationally, and seek higher education. Such transformation differed among the social classes, however. Whereas the middle and upper classes became very modern in outlook, behavior, and lifestyle, some of the poorer social segments, especially in the congested and desperately poor area of the Gaza Strip, have retained their more traditional values, organization, and social relations as have rural people. Indeed, the particularly difficult social and economic situation in the occupied territories has encouraged many to retreat into traditional kin-based networks and to religiosity and traditional values. This pattern has been aided by the emergence of more politically motivated Islamic sociopolitical organizations that have mobilized and provided some people with social services and support. In short, although some social conditions among Palestinian communities push for modernization, others continue to promote the traditional.

NOTES

1. Halim Barakat, *The Arab World* (Berkeley: University of California Press, 1988), p. 58.

2. Mahmoud Darwish, A'*ras* [Weddings] (Beirut: Dar A-Awda, 1977). Cited in ibid., p. 58.

3. Barakat, *The Arab World*, p. 115.

3

Gender, Marriage, and Family

The Palestinians have not been fortunate in achieving political independence, and thus the ability to develop public institutions that support the individual and the nuclear (small, two-generation, independent) family. Public institutions or programs such as unemployment compensation, retirement or benefits for the elderly, welfare programs, and other social safety-net programs have never been developed. Neither were private or commercial institutions such as banks that would provide long-term loans for purchasing or building homes or school loans or other such activity. Perhaps just as important, Palestinians lacked an independent economy that employed most seekers of employment with an income level that allows individuals and small nuclear families to become financially independent from other near or extended kin.

For example, conflict associated with the struggle for independence has significantly undermined the Palestinian economy of the West Bank and Gaza Strip. During the second Intifada, unemployment rates reached 60 percent in the Gaza Strip and 45 percent in the West Bank. With the Israeli siege of Palestinian cities and the restricted travel and curfews in place in 2000, these rates have increased further, and the economy practically came to a stand still. It was no different among the refugees, although the more unfortunate among them received assistance from the United Nations Relief and Works Agency (UNRWA). Accordingly, the family and the larger kin grouping remain the critical institution that sustains the individual and the small nuclear family among the Palestinians. This familial dependence became more significant after al-Nakba and accelerated further after the 1967 Arab-Israeli war and Israeli occupation. War, dispossession, displacement, occupation, migration, and forced social fragmentation have not only created greater individual and familial insecurity among Palestinians but also strengthened the need for family because there is no other source of security.

The activity of the UNRWA did help the most desperate among Palestinian refugees with basic food subsidy and elementary education for refugee camp dwellers, but it was neither sufficient for a decent standard of living nor as a basis for independence from kin. The rise and evolution of the PLO also provided non-kin-based, secular service institutions, particularly medical and educational, and, for the refugees in Lebanon, some employment. But such services reached only a fraction of the Palestinian population at any given time. Since the exit of the PLO from Beirut in the wake of the 1982 Israeli invasion of Lebanon, such PLO institutions ceased to function, and the insecurities among the refugee population have escalated significantly.

In short, given the context of Palestinian life, its attendant insecurities, its forced expulsions and social fragmentation, the family in its smaller and larger groupings continues to be the source of economic, psychological, and social security and the basis of Palestinian identity. In the course of these repeated and devastating tragedies, Palestinian families have been fragmented, transformed, and reformed to provide the needed support for the individual and the kin group. What, then, is the nature of this resilient and critical institution?

THE *'A'ILAH* AND *HAMULA* IN PALESTINE AND IN THE PALESTINIAN DIASPORA

Both traditionally and in the contemporary context, Palestinians experience and conceptualize their life not as independent individuals but as members of an extended family or *'a'ilah*. The family provides psychological, social, and economic functions to the individual. Family ties are permanent, reckoned through the male line, and characterized by mutual support, material assistance, trust, and sacrifice of the individual's interest for the greater welfare of the family. Solidarity is necessary for the effective functioning of family relations and is a strongly held value. The family is the central locus of identity and loyalty. Relations among kin are informal, extensive, and defuse, mutually supportive, reciprocal, and caring.

Nonkin relations, on the other hand, are typically more formal compared with American culture, specific, and not as trusting. Thus, social life is organized around the family in ascending order of closeness. Family and kinship relations supercede any other social relationship. Indeed, this is often why whole families and kinship groups typically are part of one political faction or another. Family and kinship are the basic institution in terms of which the individual inherits his or her identity, religious, and other social affiliations, as well as his and her social safety net.

Traditionally, in the villages and rural areas the individual lived and worked in the context of an extended family, where a patriarch with his male children and their young families holds sway. The extended family cooperated economically and in all aspects of living. Typically *'a'ilahs* or extended families of the same paternal line were and are part of a kin-based clan or *hamula*, as it is called in the villages and rural areas. Among the refugees, the 'a'ilah was often reconstituted in the camps and reemerged as the center of social life, financial cooperation, and loyalty. In fact, it was the only institution that survived, albeit transformed, the destruction of Palestine. The hamula did not fare so well; however, it did not disappear altogether.

In the West Bank and the Gaza Strip, much of village economic, political, and social life, including marriage, continues to take place within the 'a'ilah and hamula, both of which can grow quite large, with members residing in several villages or towns, or remain small, living in a small part of a single village. Classically, hamayel (plural for hamula) were the basic sociopolitical organization in the villages, towns, and rural areas of Palestine. Traditionally, large hamayel wielded political and economic power. Although they retain some of that political function and influence until today in the West Bank and Gaza Strip, the presence of the Palestinian Authority and secular political and Islamic parties have attenuated the power and influence of the hamayel except as they are linked to or are a part of the political structure. Nevertheless, in economic and social terms, the relevance of the 'a'ilah and the hamula remain strong.

The 'A'ilah

The traditional rural Palestinian extended family typically has three or more generations residing in the same household or in close proximity within a compound. The extended family shares work, income, and expenses as a single economic unit. The father (or grandfather) is the patriarch of the extended family and has the ultimate authority over all family affairs and all the members of the family and household. Besides being extended, anthropologists have characterized this family structure not only as patriarchal but also patrilineal, patrilateral, patronymic, endogamous, patrilocal, and (among some) polygamous.

This family or kinship system was traditionally the organizing principle of a stable, settled, largely subsistence-based agricultural society. This family structure, as is discussed later, transformed considerably in the second half of the nineteenth century, and particularly during the British Mandate between the two world wars. As is typical of a patriarchal society, the authority of the male head of the family is nearly absolute within the family. Authority is based on three principal criteria: gender, age, and accomplishments or position. Thus, the patriarch combines all three criteria, whereas the authority of his wife rests on the latter two criteria. Typically, she has authority over all the women and girls in the household. The eldest male child also has significant authority after the patriarch and generally becomes the head of the household with the death of his father. After gender, age is especially important in the authority structure. Experience and wisdom command respect and deference. Many proverbs instill this value in the hearts and minds of the young: for "a month older [than you], a whole generation wiser."

The Palestinian family system is patrilineal because descent is reckoned through the father, as noted earlier; it is patronymic because one's last name is derived from the father's family, clan, or *hamula*. In a village or town where one or two *hamayel* predominate, a person is typically known by his or her first name and that of the father; when the need arises, because of similarities in name a person is known by his father's and grandfather's name. Thus, a person's name could be, say, Mohammad ibn Salem (Mohammad son of Salem) without the need for reference to the clan or *hamula*. Of course, as clans or *hamayel* compete or feud or become large and spread in many localities, members of a *hamula* come to use their *hamula* name as their family or last name. Thus, in the West Bank a large number of people are named after their *hamayel*—for example, the Barghouthis, Erikats, Abdul-Hadis, Jayyusis, Masris, and many others. Typically, the firstborn male gives his own firstborn son the name of his own father. Thus, a man could be known as *Ibn* (son of) so-and-so or *Abu* (father of) so-and-so. Following the example of Mohammad ibn Salem, Mohammad, if he is the firstborn, could be referred to informally either as Ibn Salem (son of Salem) or Abu Salem (father of Salem) if he follows tradition and names his son after the name of his own father. It is a different tradition from that of the United States where people call one of their sons, usually the firstborn, by the same name as the father, not the grandfather. Thus, an American firstborn son might be called "John Smith, Jr." In Palestine, if a son is not the firstborn, he could be referred to as either, again using our example, Ibn Salem or Abu so-and-so (the name that he has given to his own firstborn son).

This family system is also considered patrilineal because the kinsmen on the father's side are considered relatives in a formal sense. This is important for many reasons. Patrilineality defines the network of relationship in which an individual is embedded and which that person needs for survival and success. In short, it defines a person's social identity. Thus, belonging to a strong patriline provides the individual with many advantages. For example, in the case of the untimely death of the father, the patrilateral relatives, typically the brother or brothers, become socially and economically responsible for the family of the deceased.

Palestinian society is considered *patrilocal* because the bride typically moves from her father's household to that of her husband's in the compound of the husband's family. There she comes under the influence of the matriarch of the family. The newly married couple thus does not reside in a separate, new household of their own (or neo-local residence as is typical in contemporary American society). For some brides, this transition is not difficult because of another feature of this extended family system: *endogamy*.

Endogamous marriage means marriage to men within the kinship group—the extended family or *hamula*. The unique feature of traditional Arab family system is the preference of endogamous marriage of a young man to his father's brother's daughter. Derivative from nomadic heritage, anthropologists call this *parallel-cousin marriage*, so labeled because the fathers of the bride and groom are brothers. This is distinct from the more common pattern in traditional tribal societies of cross-cousin marriage, marriage of a young man to his mother's brother's daughter. By custom, and not by law, in the more traditional communities the male cousin has a "claim" on his parallel cousin. Such marriages, however, are in the minority, particularly in recent history. Nevertheless, the value of endogamous marriages to kinsmen within the extended family or hamula remains strong.

Endogamy serves by combining in one practice the two kin-based values regarding descent and affinity (marriage and in-laws). For the latter reason, the father-daughter relationship is important, for it is he who decides whom she should marry and establishes relations of affinity with the family of the groom. Marriage, after all, creates an alliance and a larger kin-based grouping of two or more extended families. It thus complicates relationships that are based on patrilineal networks. Traditional marriages are typically arranged formally by the family patriarchs. They ensure that the bride and groom are socially equal members of the kin group. These kin groups or the nonkin affines may be allies or competitors in the community, the latter of which might complicate patrilineal relations.

Finally, *polygamous* marriage is allowed in Islamic law and therefore is occasionally practiced among Muslim but not Christian Palestinians. Available data shows that the incidence of polygamy is less frequent compared with endogamous marriage. Although religiously allowed, polygamous marriage is disparaged and frequently ridiculed by people in general. It is especially abhorrent to women and is a major source of conflict in the family and household. Conflict between the wives or half-brothers invariably comes to be known in the community and is a source of gossip, consternation, shame, and embarrassment for the family and kin. There are many folk proverbs and sayings that denounce and make fun of men and families that practice polygamy. Nevertheless, it serves an important social function in a traditional society that depends on sons for economic, social, and political activity and strength. Thus, if a marriage is childless or the wife does not produce sons, a husband sometimes takes a second wife in the hope of having sons. In the Palestinian social context of significant change, the practice polygamy has declined significantly.

Although formally and typically patriarchal, women do play a significant role within the Palestinian family system—so much so that in many families, the mother or grandmother plays a unifying, even dominant role in family affairs. The real nucleus of many families may in fact be the elder sister or grandmother, whose home is always open for family gatherings—morning coffee, afternoon tea, and lunches.

As the matriarch of a family, a woman often plays a leadership role; she is asked for advice and assistance and to arbitrate disputes. Thus, despite the patriarchal structure of many families—nuclear and extended—many are actually matriarchal. In the tragic experience of al-Nakba, many mothers or grandmothers had to raise their children (or grandchildren) single-handedly after a husband or son died. As Palestinians lost everything to Israel during 1948, many widowed or separated women had to work, raise their children, and keep the family going in exile. They were remarkable women known for their strength, wisdom, and tolerance. Those women often emerged as respected matriarchs. Cultural traditions can adapt readily to changed and traumatic conditions.

The Functionally Extended Family

The *'a'ilah* in the villages and towns has suffered extensive transformation as a result of al-Nakba, including the social fragmentation of communities and Palestinian migration. Israeli occupation of the West Bank and Gaza Strip has also played a role, transforming the traditional economy into a market economy and thus leading to the development of a labor market. These factors have brought about the "functionally extended family" in place of the extended family. Whereas in the extended family, the individual and nuclear family units reside, work, and live together in patriarchal compounds in the village, in the functionally extended family, the nuclear family unit resides separately, sometimes on different continents and works separately, but the individual and extended units continue to provide economic, financial, and other support to each other.

For example, a large number of men (some with nuclear family units) from the Occupied Territories and the refugee camps in the neighboring Arab countries have migrated to work in the labor-poor oil-producing Arab countries of the Arabian Peninsula. They send much of their income to the family and kin that they left behind. It has been estimated that nearly 50 percent of the West Bank gross national product came from remittances from Palestinian expatriate workers. This changed when Kuwait, in the wake of the 1991 Gulf War, expelled about 400,000 Palestinians from a community of some 450,000 who had been resident in Kuwait for nearly 40 years; the Kuwaiti government was displeased by the position that 'Arafat and the PLO took in regard to the Iraqi occupation of Kuwait.

In the urban centers and among the middle class, the Palestinians continue to live in functionally extended families both in the West Bank and the Gaza Strip, as well as in diaspora communities. As in the rural areas, the lack of public and private support institutions and the insecure economic conditions have mandated the continued importance of the family and kin for the survival and success of the individual. Here, too, individual access to paid employment, government and nongovernmental organization services, professional services, education, and training are typically mediated through family connections and networks. Help and financial support is often rendered across countries and continents. Older retired parents are completely dependent on their families and would not survive without direct financial, caregiving, emotional, and moral support of the adult children. Accordingly, these connections and social functions reinforce family solidarity and loyalty among all Palestinian social classes.

The community is really an extension of the family. Familial events, such as weddings, births, deaths, and religious holidays, are occasions for the entire family, *hamula*, and community to pause and either celebrate or mourn together. Visitors from other places are great occasions for a break in routine of everyday life, and everyone comes to pay their respects, both upon the visitors' arrival and their pending departure. Visitors also provide outside information about other family members and friends and about happenings in other parts of the world. As can be imagined, this was much more important in the past, before the increased availability of telephones and television and new technologies such as satellites and the Internet.

Tolerance in families and communities is high. Idiosyncrasies are easily overlooked or forgiven. People with handicaps are cared for within the family and often communally. Elders are valued and respected for their knowledge and wisdom. There are also unwritten codes of behavior and family honor that bind family and community. The face of social relationships must be preserved at all costs. Other members of the family mediate differences and conflicts; once achieved, the public face of resolution is staunchly maintained, even if ill feelings remain. Divorce is frowned upon, and family members intervene to prevent it whenever possible.

Family Life Cycle

Like all cultures, the Palestinians have unique rites of passage or life cycle celebrations and rituals. When a baby is born, especially a boy, much celebration takes place in the family and among the extended kin. Well-wishers come to the house to congratulate the parents and grandparents. They are typically served coffee, tea, and *mughli*—a pudding made of semolina flour, sugar, and cinnamon, topped with fresh nuts, especially almonds with their skins removed. The celebrations and congratulations for a new birth may last several weeks.

Another important celebration is the ritual of baptism for Palestinian Christians, a ritual that differs among various Christian sects. Among the Orthodox Christians, the most numerous among the Palestinians, the infant is immersed into the baptismal bath. Another important event for Orthodox Christians and eastern Catholics, is confirmation, which takes place at age seven.

The next important rite of passage is at puberty. Muslim girls in villages and some urban areas were long encouraged to cover (veil) their heads at puberty; this is still the case among the more traditional of the population. Among some traditional Muslim families, boys at puberty are circumcised. After puberty, the most important event is a couple's wedding. Wedding ceremonies were traditionally elaborate, involving not only the family and extended kin, but often the whole village and clansmen from other villages. Today, wedding ceremonies in diaspora communities are modest because many kinsmen and village community members have been dispersed and because of cost of travel. In urban centers, Palestinian weddings are still elaborate, but they involve fewer people because the clan and community links are more modest in number.

Traditional wedding ceremonies last three days, sometimes more. The celebrations at the homes of both the bride and groom are extensive. Among the Muslims, the marriage ceremony takes place at two distinct times: at the writing and signing of the marriage contract and at another celebration that marks the actual consummation of the marriage. In villages, the bride is literally carried to the home of the groom in a parade. The celebrations during the parade and at the home of the groom are usually joyful and gay, with music, dancing, and singing and the enjoyment of much food and sweets. Typically, one or more lambs are slaughtered for the occasion. Members of the extended family and *hamula* prepare other dishes. All the people attending the wedding celebrations march behind the bride or congregate at the home of the groom, sitting in a grand circle around the living room and other open spaces, drinking and eating and either watching or participating in dances. The bride may actually do a solo dance, typically slow, rhythmic, and graceful. After the bridal dance, relatives and friends, both men and women, often compete with each other in dancing to the rhythm and drum beat and clapping. Such public communal weddings bind the community and assert its traditional values, norms, and customs. In urban centers, the weddings are typically more private and involve the family, the functionally extended family, neighbors, and friends.

As with the joyful wedding celebrations, funerals in Palestinian villages also bring together extended kin and the *hamula*. Kinsmen, friends, and dignitaries sit facing each other in a circle, sip unsweetened bitter coffee, and whisper conversations among themselves, often about the life and qualities of the deceased. Customs in Palestine require the family to mourn the dead for at least forty days, during which the women wear black clothing and the men wear a black tie and sometimes a black band around the arm. A widow or a mother may wear black for at least one year, and sometimes three. These traditions are common among both Muslim and Christian Palestinians. Islamic tradition in Palestine and elsewhere requires that the dead be buried quickly, within 24 hours.

Patriarchy, Values, and the Code of Family Honor

As noted earlier, the traditional Palestinian ethics of family relations and many societal institutions are patriarchal. Duties and obligations are defined in the family and other institutions of society along lines dictated by gender. The ideology of "complementarity"[1] legitimized the social hierarchy. Complementarity specifies that although roles, duties, and responsibilities are dissimilar, they are idealized as reciprocal, and therefore equal and legitimate in the eyes of the family, society, and within both the Christian and Muslim religious discourses. Although objectively unequal, this belief is not unlike in most traditional societies in which the roles of men and women are distinctively defined. The structure of patriarchy places men, especially older men, in privileged and powerful position over the life and well-being of women and the family as a whole. They are, however, obligated to be the providers, protectors, and leaders of the family and *hamula*.

Traditionally, patriarchy was upheld by a value and discourse of honor (*sharaf* or *'ard*). The honor and reputation of the family and its women was traditionally a very important status to uphold. Often, however, this family honor was defined narrowly as domain in the family's women, who were expected to exhibit modesty in demeanor and dress, self-restraint, self-effacement, sexual chastity before marriage and fidelity after, and obedience to male guardians, husbands, and elders.

The norms of upholding *sharaf* include, for men and women, not speaking ill of family members or discussing family affairs with nonkin. This was important because the family and kin, particularly the *hamayel*, were not only social and economic organizations but political ones as well. Familial discord that is made known to people outside the kin group could undermine the political power and influence of the family. Accordingly, the norm was to keep any discord internal to the family and secret from outsiders.

In the wake of al-Nakba and in the context of Israeli occupation, the process of political mobilization and the secular organizations of resistance introduced alternative structures of responsibility and support, provided more modern roles and role models for refugee camp dwellers, encouraged women to enter the labor market, promoted the development of non-kin-based service organization, and redefined honor as the service in the cause of the people of Palestine. Thus, these social factors began the process of challenging and dismantling the traditional patriarchy. The more recent evolution of political Islamic and resistance organizations, however, has undermined secular, non-kin-based trends, especially in the Gaza Strip and some parts of the West Bank. This has reinforced traditional structures of patriarchy and social organization. In short, varied patterns of change and transformation in family values, norms of behavior, and the patterns of relations within varied Palestinian communities indicate that these aspects of family life are in flux.

Marriage Patterns

Traditionally, marriage between a young man and a young woman in rural areas of Palestine was arranged by the fathers (or guardians) of the bride and groom. Although the women in the family played a crucial role in the informal process of bringing the two parties together, the formal ceremonies were presided over by the male guardians. This was the pattern among both Muslim and Christian Palestinians of rural areas. Often these were parallel-cousin marriage. This traditional Arabic pattern had its origins in the desert pre-Islamic nomadic tribal lifestyle and has survived as a preference in much of the Arab World. It also seems to have remained fairly prevalent among the refugee camp communities and villages of the West Bank and Gaza Strip. In a survey conducted by the Palestinian Central Bureau of Statistics in 1995, first-cousin marriages comprised 27.5 percent of all marriages of those between the ages of 15 and 54, with parallel-cousin marriage making up 24.4 percent of these. More dramatic, marriages within the same *hamula* represented 58 percent of all marriages in villages and 43.5 percent in refugee camps of the West Bank and Gaza Strip.[2] These patterns and rates of marriage are likely to be much lower in refugee camps in neighboring Arab countries and among the diaspora in general, especially the middle class. *Hamayel* in those countries are generally not intact, and the impact of secular political movements on social organization has been strong. Today marriage to nonkin is more common and often preferred among the middle classes.

In cities and larger towns, traditional marriage patterns were varied before al-Nakba. Although a small fraction were arranged, among the middle and upper classes, two individuals would typically be introduced to each other by kin; they would then court under family supervision for nine months to two years before deciding to get married. A smaller fraction among the more modern social classes followed a pattern closer to that of the West; individuals chose their marriage partner, typically based on love.

The tragedies and challenges of Palestinian life over the last three generations—"war, dispossession, social fragmentation, displacement, foreign rule, and political, social and economic insecurity"[3]—have brought about important changes in the structure and dynamics of family life for most Palestinians. These changes have affected residence patterns, norms of behavior for women, values and codes governing relations between husbands and wives and among kinsmen, child-rearing practices, and marriage patterns. Not least in impact is the extended absence of husbands who work in other countries, who have been imprisoned by the Israeli occupation authorities, or who have been maimed in the long and convoluted Palestinian struggle for freedom and independence.

Although marriage patterns in the Occupied Territories remain strongly traditional in character, among the rest of the Palestinian population, they are not. The best way to comprehend the contemporary Palestinian marriage patterns is to imagine their pattern of distribution on a statistical, bell-shaped curve. On the left side of the bell are a large minority of all marriages, which are traditional with a preference for kinsmen. The right side of the bell, a more-or-less equal segment to that on the left, represents marriage by individual choice. The middle of the curve, perhaps a plurality, represents marriages in which the partners are introduced to each other by kinsmen or friends or meet in a public place (such as school or work), court for a period of time, and then marry with the approval and support of their respective families. This predominant pattern is somewhere between individual choice and arranged marriage. Finally, as a result of exile and dispersion, Palestinians have more than ever intermarried with other nationalities and religious, ethnic, and other groups. Mixed marriages are most common among Palestinians who live in Europe and the Americas and among the most educated. Among the middle and educated social classes, especially those Palestinians living in Europe and the Americas, the patterns of courtship and the choice of a marriage partner are not very different from those of Westerners.

If the prospective bride and groom come to know each other through family, friends, school, or work and the future groom indicates seriousness of purpose, then a process is typically begun. The bride's family will inquire about the young suitor and his family if both are unknown to them. The inquiry is quite informal and seeks information about the health, well-being, character, and wealth and occupation of the prospective groom and the general reputation of his family. With the suitor's intentions well known to the bride's family, the father of the bride typically asks her what she wants to do. If she is in favor of the possible marriage to the young suitor, her father will initiate formal contact with the family (father) of the prospective groom. If she is unsure and wants to think about it or to get to know the prospective groom better, a series of meetings in the form of a preengagement courtship, often with a chaperone, take place. Depending on the degree of traditionalism of the family, the father will agree to give his daughter the freedom to meet the prospective bridegroom alone or with a chaperone and as much time as she needs to make her decision. The groom's visits may take place at the home of the bride in her family's living room where the prospective suitors are left alone.

Upon making her decision to marry the young suitor, the father of the bride will ask again if this is what she really wants to do. If the bride's answer is positive, the young suitor is informed, and the formal part of the process of marriage follows. The father of the groom will typically come to the family of the bride and ask, on behalf of his son, for the hand of the potential bride in marriage. Based on that willingness between the two parties, the two fathers discuss the *muhur* (dowry) for the bride. The *muhur* is set in accordance with the social status of the two families. Among the working classes, it could reach as high as 1,000 to 2,000 Jordanian dinars ($5,000–6,000). The bride may also receive gold jewelry including rings, bracelets, necklaces, and so on. The prospective bride receives the *muhur* from the future groom to do with as she pleases, often choosing to buy items for her trousseau. This amount of money is basically symbolic and is similar to the diamond ring that a prospective bride receives from her fiancé in the United States. Formal marriage agreements in the Islamic tradition are very much like a marriage contract. Thus, as a *muhur* is set so is the *mo'akhar*. The *mo'akhar* is the amount due the wife from the husband in case of a divorce, which can be symbolic or as extensive as the two parties deem appropriate. There is no specific money exchanged for the *mo'akhar* at the time of engagement or marriage.

After the bride receives the *muhur*, a small celebration typically takes place, attended by most immediate family members on both sides. Next, a larger party is held where engagement rings are exchanged. The bride usually will have had her special ring and special robe or dress made for the occasion. All of the family and friends—sometimes hundreds of people—are typically present. Usually such parties are held at home, but some well-to-do families might have the party at a hotel. Food and drink are available, and the people at the party dance the *Dabke* (a communal dance, described in chapter 7); there is also belly dancing, shoulder shaking, and other dance forms. After a few months of courting, the wedding date is set.

Following their engagement party, the couple may go out to a late dinner together, among some family members, alone, or with a family member from the bride's side who acts as a chaperone. After the period of courting that may last from a few months to a year or even two, the young couple agree to go to the Islamic *Shari'a* (religious) court to complete the marriage. At the court, the judge asks if the bride wants to be married to her fiancé. (If she says no, this will be the end of the process.) The written marriage contract specifying the *muhur* and the *mo'akhar* is signed in front of the judge by both individuals. Then another small party is held with the family. Next, a wedding ceremony, marked by another large party, at home or in a hotel, takes place; as in the West, the bride typically wears a white wedding gown. Food, music, dancing, and a layered wedding cake are common features of such celebrations. After this party, the bride and her husband usually go to a hotel (if the groom can afford it) to start their honeymoon. Shortly thereafter, the bride and groom go to their new home. In most urban populations, the two have their separate home (neo-local residence). In smaller towns and villages and among the more traditional families, the two reside in the home of the family of the groom (patrilocal residence), usually in semiseparate quarters.

The patterns among the Palestinian Christians of the same class status and level of traditionalism do not differ significantly. Not unlike the Western Christians, a church wedding would be planned and the marriage sealed. There is no civil marriage among the Palestinians, nor in most traditions of the Middle East, including the Israelis. All marriages take place in ecclesiastical or religious contexts. Thus, marriage and divorce laws are those of the respective churches. Accordingly, divorce laws vary by the respective ecclesiastical courts. Among Muslims, divorce is allowed, but among the varieties of Palestinian (and other Arab) Catholics, divorce is not permitted, only annulment, which is a very difficult process. Orthodox Christians, however, allow divorce under extremely limited conditions.

The factors responsible for familial solidarity and the endogamous family and *hamula* marriage patterns, described earlier, are also responsible for the low divorce rate among Palestinians. The enormous stress under which Palestinians have been living since 1948 have, however, generated numerous psychological and social problems that have put tremendous strain on family life. Few scientific studies document and analyze the consequences of severe stress on Palestinian families, but anecdotal evidence has shown an increase in domestic conflict and violence, and probably divorce as well.

Child Rearing

The extended and functionally extended families in the context of which most Palestinians live are characterized by a strong and enduring bond of familial solidarity and loyalty. The formal and informal social and affective functions that families provide for their members are important to producing such loyalty. Therefore, the socialization processes of children underlie these functions. In contrast to child-rearing patterns in the United States where children are placed on a structured and controlled routine of daily activity—breakfast time, play time, naptime, lunchtime, and so on until bedtime—the daily life cycle of Palestinian children is not structured at all. Typically, the infant or child is fed, allowed to play, rest, or nap at its own pace and pleasure. A newborn, especially if it is a male, becomes the center of attention, care, and love of the extended or functionally extended family. Older siblings join in the showering of attention, care, and love for the newborn. The infant or child feels as if he or she is at the center of the world. Indeed, it is this constant early attention and stroking that cements individual self-esteem as well as the bond to kin.

As should be clear, when family members live in close proximity, social inter-action among kinsmen is frequent, daily, and multifaceted. The family and its extensions are central to a person's social and economic well-being. Various adults will praise and discipline the children. Conversations are not segregated, so children are very much a part of every topic and issue. When family and friends visit, children often greet the guests at the door and shake hands with everyone who comes. They sit with the adults and often assist in the serving of coffee or sweets. They overhear and sometimes participate in family gossip and the dilemmas and triumphs of family members and the family as a whole.

Child rearing in the United States is oriented to producing independent indi-viduals as early as possible; in contrast, among Palestinians it is oriented to creat-ing an individual with a strong family bond, attachment, loyalty, and collective responsibility. A close bond especially develops between the mother and her chil-dren, in particular, the firstborn male. The extensive and extended closeness, love, and caring generates in a child an enduring and strong attachment to the family and kin. This is a logical development because of the centrality of the fam-ily in the individual's life, and made even more important given the insecure con-text of Palestinian life, particularly since al-Nakba and the occupation. It has been noted that

West Bank camp and village families are the primary providers of the individual members' material and emotional needs—identity, marriage, work, shelter, clothing, moral guid-ance, affection—family members must be socialized not only to assume their proper roles and obligations, but also to place family interests before any individual needs, desires or interests. Children must be taught that their futures are inextricably bound up in other peoples' perception of their family's reputation just as thoroughly as she is responsible for it. The fear of tarnishing the family image is a strong inducement to self-control for chil-dren of all ages.[4]

The eldest male is typically expected to provide for and help aging parents in their retirement. Typically, the aging parents—the patriarch and the matriarch—reside in the home of the eldest male, who also carries the family leadership role and the name of the family. This is one aspect of family honor and obligation that resides in the eldest male. In reality, this pattern differs among families depend-ing on the presence and ability of the eldest or other male children to look after the aging parents. If no male children exist, female children typically take up the responsibility.

Market researchers and marketers in the West have discovered what a huge and easily impressionable market segment exists among teens and young adults. Youth in Palestine and diaspora communities are no less susceptible to those advertising campaigns and influences. In the West, sex sells, and the youth are bombarded with media-created images that promote and encourage situations, behaviors, and activities in conflict with the cultural values and lifestyle of the people. Accordingly, such influences introduce elements of tension and conflict among youth and their parents or guardians. This, along with education, has had a strong impact on Palestinian youth, especially middle-class youth in diaspora communities and in the major cities in the West Bank and, to a lesser extent, the Gaza Strip. The impact of external influences to the family has become a key factor in changing the mores, norms, and behavior patterns of youth, including young women, and their relationship to their family and kin.

Intrafamily patterns of gender relations are also changing. Traditionally the boy or young man in the family is more privileged, especially if he has sisters and, in better off families, a maid. The boys do less housework and have greater social freedoms (e.g., later parentally enforced curfews) than girls. In many educated and cosmopolitan families, girls are treated the same as boys, however. Parents expect and encourage daughters to stand on their own two feet, stressing education as the only thing they can count on in life. Many professional Palestinian women today wonder whether parents would have emphasized their daughters' self-reliance if they had not been living in exile, without the security of a homeland. It is likely that these parents would have, particularly if both were highly educated, because even before al-Nakba, Palestine was in the throes of modernization and the emergence of a market economy.

THE CHANGING ROLE OF WOMEN

The private and public role of Palestinian women has been changing dramatically since al-Nakba and as a result of the prolonged Israeli occupation, although there is great diversity among Palestinians in this regard—customs in the tribes of the desert plains versus customs of the hill country agrarian populations; the Bedouin lifestyle versus that of the village versus that of the city. Various other factors affect Palestinian women's roles as well, such as social class, education, and religious tradition. Differences related to these factors, among many others, can be extensive and are now exacerbated by the degree of exposure to Europeans and Americans through interactions in their own country or through television, travel, expatriate living, or educational opportunities.

Traditionally, a Palestinian woman's role was to be a wife, mother, and family caregiver. Within peasant and farming communities, women worked their home gardens and tended farm animals; they also worked the fields, especially during harvest. In many respects, their role was not different from that of women on farms in the pre–World War I United States. Yet whereas educational and labor market involvement and achievement have been the principal factors pushing for change in the status of U.S. women, al-Nakba and the problems derived from Israeli occupation have been the most important factors among their Palestinian counterparts. Al-Nakba led to a loss of economic resources—land and busi-

Women in Ramallah. © E. Y. Farsakh

nesses—and therefore to the means to earn a living. Most male Palestinian refugees (former peasants and farmers) were suddenly forced to seek employment in their host countries or in the West Bank and the Gaza Strip. Work was either unavailable or insufficient to provide for a family. Accordingly, many women were compelled to enter the labor market in different capacities to supplement the family income. Poor, illiterate women, especially widows, from the villages and camps, often had little option but to work in low-status occupations (including wage labor in commercial agriculture or house, hospital, and office cleaning) for low wages.

Both al-Nakba and the occupation have pushed more and more Palestinians off the farm and into wage labor, a social phenomenon or process called *proletarianization* by social scientists. On one hand, the underdeveloped Palestinian economy has restricted opportunities for women among the peasant and working classes because of poverty, lack of education and employment opportunities, early marriage, and high fertility rates. On the other hand, the very same lack of development led to migration of men to the oil-producing states in search of work; the resultant labor scarcity, together with economic need, often compelled women to seek employment to enhance family income. In between the periods of the two Intifadas, many women even went to work in Israel, principally in menial jobs that paid poorly. Others worked as seamstresses for garment subcontractors of Israeli firms. Women were favored in this kind of work in many underdeveloped countries because they are considered productive, docile, and inexpensive workers. Typically they are paid less, according to a clearly divergent wage system from that of men. This leads to exploitation because women have fewer job options. Basically, then, in the occupied West Bank and Gaza Strip, there has been a shift in women's work from artisan production and farm work to industrial subcontracting. The paradox is that these women have also come out of the traditional mold of a women's role as a wife and mother. Furthermore, "numerous women became heads of households when their husbands left the country to seek work or when they were imprisoned or deported for political activism."[5]

What has also helped Palestinian women enter the paid labor force in a variety of occupations is the education that many received in the UNRWA schools in the refugee camps and in private schools for the middle classes. Education is extremely valued by the Palestinian people. In the diaspora communities, both men and women have had to rely on their education and their skilled workmanship to secure economic well-being. It is a given that women of the middle and upper classes will complete high school and go on to universities. Whenever possible, postgraduate work is encouraged as well. It is assumed that most of these women will then work after graduation. No less significant is education for Palestinians under occupation in the West Bank and the Gaza Strip.

In the thirty some years of occupation since 1967, the Palestinians in the Occupied Territories have established several universities to educate their people, especially those who cannot afford to go abroad for higher education. In 1992–93 in the Occupied Territories, women comprised about 35 percent of all university students.[6] "Today Palestinian women at all (social) levels work outside the home, most in unskilled jobs, but others in highly skilled positions. . . . In a shift in attitudes that would have been unimaginable fifty years ago . . . college-educated women have been able to enter the public workforce with little opposition—in fact, generally with encouragement—from the men in their families."[7] In the West Bank, 49 percent of the nonagricultural female labor force were in professional positions by 1972.[8]

Women in historic Palestine—Israel and the Occupied Territories—and in the diaspora communities have entered practically all the professions: teaching, medicine, dentistry, pharmacy, engineering, law, accounting, auditing, and others. Furthermore, among expatriate communities in the oil-producing Gulf States, opportunities in the labor market also encouraged Palestinian women to enter the labor force in various white-collar occupations because native women of those countries lived within even more traditional and conservative contexts. "Upper- and upper-middle-class Palestinian women (particularly urban women) enjoy considerable autonomy with regard to decisions in such areas as education, employment, age at marriage, and number of children, village and camp women have far fewer choices."[9] If a married woman works, there are many hands to help make the logistics of her life tolerable. Although the burden of running the household is still fully on women, whether they work outside the home or not, they do receive assistance from extended family members, who care for the children and assist with shopping, meal preparation, and other household duties. The familial support system allows women a feeling of security and increases solidarity among the extended kin.

Particularly among the Palestinian refugees, the secular Palestinian political movement under the banner of the PLO, has also encouraged women to break out of the traditional role and strike out into new social, political, and economic directions. Among the guerilla groups that comprised the military wing of component parts of the PLO, women also became guerilla fighters and engaged in resistance to Israeli incursions and invasions, especially in Lebanon. Palestinian women

have taken an ever-increasing role in politics, especially in the West Bank and Gaza Strip, where the Israeli occupation since 1967 has altered traditional patterns, and many women from all strata of society have joined in political resistance. In the territories, a network of women's organizations with several thousand members, and a base of support in all cities and in most villages and camps, has grown increasingly influential in Palestinian public life.[10]

Compared to how they are portrayed in the West, Palestinian women often have more significance and power in their society and in family units; in some ways they have greater influence than their Western counterparts. Their role in the first Intifada against Israeli occupation is well documented.[11] The family is valued above all else; thus, because women are at the center of the family and serve as the preservationists, they hold an undisputed position of strength. Communal values back up this role. Palestinian women are extremely proficient at using their knowledge of this position of influence—they recognize, understand, and regularly utilize it in ways that strengthen the values of their society and their family, their resistance to occupation, and this ultimately provides them with a quality of life that they cherish.

In short, the role and status of Palestinian women has been transforming dramatically over the years. They have not only entered the workforce, both in their homeland and their refugee host countries, they have also emerged as active participants in the political and public life of their society—in social service organizations and in political movements and parties. The contexts have changed over the years and among the various Palestinian communities, but in large measure, the traditional mold of women's role has been broken. Now, despite the difficult conditions under which they and their families live, Palestinian women are poised to undergo greater role change than ever before.

One aspect of Muslim women's status that is played up in Western media and academia is the role of the veil in women's public dress. The wearing of various types of veil (e.g., head veils those covering the face) by Muslim women has been on the decline in Palestine since World War I but especially after al-Nakba. One of the strongest influences that helped eliminate veil wearing among the Palestinians was the rise of secular political movements, especially among diaspora communities. The women of the upper and middle classes and the more educated families have discarded the veil altogether. Among the other classes, especially the peasants and farmers and other villagers, the head veil continues to be practiced along with traditional dress. However, one interesting contradiction to note is that the rise in the last 20 years of the Islamic political movements among Palestinians under Israeli occupation has encouraged the wearing of the veil in some communities. While helping the poor through nongovernmental philanthropic organizations, the Islamic movements have simultaneously encouraged conservative social values and behavior while increasing their political and armed resistance against the occupation. Thus, the traditional dress and behavior patterns were reasserted among certain sectors of the population, leading to a rise in veiling. The end of occupation and a solution to the Palestinian-Israeli conflict coupled with a growing economy would probably reintroduce the secular and modernistic trends that existed before. Veiling, like other social practices, is a phenomenon that is influenced by social, economic and political factors.

In surveys and anecdotal evidence reported in newspaper interviews, women often indicate that they wear the head veil voluntarily. Some more traditional fathers and families pressure the young woman after puberty to wear it; others do not and leave it to the woman's choice. Typically, if the mother and older sisters are veiled, then a young woman typically will choose to wear one as well, especially among the Palestinians of the villages and small towns in occupied regions. Wearing the veil among Palestinian women has varied motivations. Some do so because of religious belief, others as a sign of identity, still others as a sign of defiance to the Israeli occupiers. Those who are religious often indicate that they are more comfortable wearing the veil in public because it protects them against unwanted advances by strange men. They feel more secure socially and are able to maneuver in public without any problems. After the September 11, 2001, attacks, Muslim women in the United States and Europe—including Palestinians—have reported hostile looks and verbal abuse when they wear the veil in public, a direct contrast to the respect accorded them in the Arab World.

NOTES

1. Cheryl Rubenberg, *Palestinian Women: Patriarchy and Resistance* (Boulder, CO: Lynne Rienner, 2001), p. 40.

2. Ibid., p. 33.

3. Ibid., p. 73.

4. Ibid., p. 76.

5. Ibid.

6. Government of Israel, Central Bureau of Statistics, *Statistical Abstract of Israel*, 2000, pp. 830–31.

7. Michael Gorkin and Rafiqa Othman, *Three Mothers, Three Daughters: Palestinian Women's Stories* (Berkeley: University of California Press, 1996), p. 4.

8. Annelies Moors, *Women, Property and Islam: Palestinian Experiences, 1920–1990* (Cambridge: Cambridge University Press, 1995), p. 230.

9. Rubenberg, *Palestinian Women*, p. 56.

10. Gorkin and Othman, *Three Mothers, Three Daughters*, p. 5. See also Orayb Najjar, *Portraits of Palestinian Women* (Salt Lake City: University of Utah Press, 1992); and Kitty Warnock, *Land before Honour* (New York: Monthly Review Press, 1990).

11. See Joost Hilterman, *Behind the Intifada: Labor and Women's Movements in the Occupied Territories* (Princeton, NJ: Princeton University Press, 1981); and Phillipa Strum, *The Women Are Marching: The Second Sex and the Palestinian Revolution* (Chicago: Lawrence Hill Books, 1992).

4

Traditional Dress and Cuisine

Palestine, like all traditional societies in the world, has developed distinctive styles of dress and cuisine, two features that are important in any culture. To some degree, these aspects of Palestinian culture are shared with the Arab peoples of neighboring countries. Nevertheless, Palestinians have developed some of these traditions into very distinctive aspects, none more than the embroidered dresses of women—both peasants and urbanites. This chapter reviews not only the traditional dress and cuisine of the Palestinian people but also their contemporary transformations.

TRADITIONAL GARMENTS AND THEIR MODERN TRANSFORMATIONS

Palestinians share many aspects of their traditional dress with the Arabs of nearby countries. Nevertheless, they have unique and distinctive features that distinguish their garments, costumes, headdresses, and veils from those of surrounding countries. The dress of both men and women, especially in the cities, was also influenced over the years by the urban elite, and by the ruling Turkish classes, and then by the British during the Mandate. Village dress remained largely immune to the imported styles; however, it occasionally incorporated some stylistic features of these foreign influences. Styles of dress and the decorative features varied by place of residence, social organization, and lifestyle, whether urban, village, or nomadic Bedouin. Remarkably, even in the diaspora refugee camps, the Palestinian women in particular have preserved, reproduced, and expanded the use of traditional decorative styles and techniques. Indeed, a cottage industry in the preservation and expansion of the unique Palestinian

style of decoration—embroidery—has evolved in the refugee camps of the occupied territories and in the Arab host countries of Lebanon, Syria, and Jordan.

Men's Traditional Garments

Men's garments varied not only by urban, village, and nomadic lifestyle but
also by identity, status (descent or wealth), and age. In the rural and nomadic
areas, men typically wore a tunic that was generally white or indigo blue cotton
or wool manufactured locally on handlooms. This changed progressively during
the British Mandate period into a long shirt that was tailored in European style.
The tunic was covered during the colder months by an 'abayah—a large, loose,
ankle-length overcoat, typically made of wool for warmth. Many also wore baggy
pants called *shirwal*. Of Turkish origin, *shirwals* were pants that were tight-fitting
on the lower legs but wide at the hips and waist, where they were gathered in
folds by a sting or belt. As with the tunic, the 'abayah was abandoned for a calf-
or ankle-length coat with narrow sleeves. The coats were of simple cotton. Fine
silk coats, richly decorated and better tailored, were worn by wealthier men for
special occasions, such as weddings or religious celebrations.

By the time of the Mandate, European-style coats replaced all others in both
cities and villages, where they were worn over the more contemporary village
tunics or *qumbaz*. Whereas villagers adopted a more functional style of dress,
urban Palestinians began to wear European trousers and jackets by the end of the
nineteenth century, a style that has become more widely used by all sectors of
Palestinian society since the Mandate and continues today in the West Bank,
Gaza Strip, and in diaspora communities.

Traditional Palestinian men wore leather sandals or went barefoot if they were
very poor. Horsemen, however, wore red or yellow soft leather boots made locally.
Footwear was considered unclean, and thus sandals, boots, and shoes were
removed before entering the house. Traditional headwear was clearly marked
according to whether the men were urban dwellers, villagers, or Bedouins. Headwear, through size, shape, and color, also indicated a person's religious affiliation,
wealth, and sociopolitical position. In cities, traditional Palestinians wore the
Turkish red *tarbush*, often referred to as fez, a stiff felt hat shaped like an small
upturned pail with a black tassel. In villages, men's headwear varied considerably
in style, color, and size—typically, a soft, round, red felt hat with a navy blue tassel or a *laffeh*, a cloth wrap that forms a turban. The greater the size of the *laffeh*
and turban, the more important, wealthy, and powerful the person. *Laffeh* colors
also indicated the religious affiliation and position of the wearer. For example,
large white turbans were typically worn by Sunni Muslim religious judges, or *qadis*.

Palestinian Bedouins wore headwear that distinguished them from villagers
and urbanites. The Bedouin headdress comprised a square cloth (*hattah* or *kaffiyyeh*) folded diagonally over the head and held in place with black ropes (*'egal*)
made of goat or camel hair. The *hatta* or *kaffiyyeh* were made of cotton or fine
wool and were either white or white with black or red designs. This Bedouin

Kaffiyyeh and jacket. © E. Y. Farsakh

headdress allowed the person to cover most of the face except the eyes, which could be shielded with the cloth during sandstorms. Beginning in the 1930s, a significant and symbolic change took place among villagers and townsmen, as well as some urban dwellers. The *hatta* and *'egal* headdress became a symbol of Palestinian nationalism and was thus adopted for headwear by many rural and town Palestinians of most all classes. Indeed, the distinctive black-and-white *kaffiyyeh* by the contemporary Palestinian leader Yasser 'Arafat became an international symbol of Palestinian identity and nationalism. Nowadays, young and old wear this headdress, or scarves made of the same color and design, to assert their Palestinian identity and loyalty to the cause of Palestine. The black-and-white design of the *kaffiyyeh* often appears on political posters, paintings, cartoons, book covers, and other graphic designs that express Palestinian history, politics, and identity. Many Europeans and Americans, especially students, wear the *kaffiyyeh* as a sign of support for the Palestinian cause. Generally, however, in the three principal contemporary Palestinian communities—inside Israel, under occupation, and in exile—men of all classes wear European-style clothing, under-garments, shoes, and often even European hats.

Women's Traditional Garments

Women's garments, especially festive costumes, were—and among women in the West Bank villages and refugee camps still are—far more diverse and elaborately decorated than men's. The extensive variety of women's costumes is based largely on the color, fabric, and structure of designs and especially the embroidery employed to embellish dresses, costumes, jackets, headdresses, and other accessories. Embroidery is common to many cultures and societies in eastern Mediterranean countries, but among Palestinian village and nomadic Bedouin women, it is an art form. "Palestinian embroidery with its bold repeated, balanced compositions and vivid and harmonious combinations of color, certainly has a character entirely and unmistakably its own."[1] Indeed, it is so distinctive and unique that it has become a principal symbol of Palestinian identity and heritage in the wake of al-Nakba. Nowadays, women of all social classes, lifestyles, and sophistication purchase such embroidered dresses for evening and formal wear and for decorating their homes both in the occupied territories and in the Palestinian diaspora communities.

Traditionally, embroidered dresses and coats were an essential part of a young woman's marriage trousseau. She would learn to embroider, mastering stitches, techniques, styles, and aesthetic standards—from her mother, elder siblings, aunts, and other kin. This typically begins early, with the young woman often embroidering pieces of her wedding trousseau even before puberty. For everyday use, dresses were lightly embroidered. The most elaborately and lavishly decorated embroidered dress usually was the young woman's wedding dress. The trousseau, however, had several more embroidered dresses, coats, jackets, shawls, and head veils (scarves that cover a woman's hair, not her face), and other accessories, a mattress (*firash*), a quilt (*ilhaf*), and embroidered cushion covers, most of which were stored in a chest that the woman would take with her to her new home with her husband. The trousseau also included jewelry and a headdress adorned with coins in gold or silver given to the bride by her father and typically draped around and attached to the front of her wedding headdress over which a large embroidered head veil was worn. The marriage ceremonies were elaborate, involved practically all the relatives and the whole village, and took place over several days. These ceremonies, which had their own rituals, routines, and rhythm, were all festive and important social occasions, and, like holidays and religious festivals, reinforced the bonding and solidarity of the village folk.

Through style, stitch, color of dress, and the structure and colors of embroidery, traditional garments and costumes indicated whether a woman was a Bedouin, villager, or townswoman. More specifically, women's clothing indicated the village, region, or Bedouin tribe to which she belonged. Styles also differed among social classes and among those groups that were distant from each other geographically. On the other hand, they were more similar, with nuanced differences, among socially and geographically close groups. Thus, traditional Palestinian styles of embroidery emerged, clustered in groups of villages in different subregions of the country. Nonetheless, as Shelagh Weir, who authored two books on Palestinian embroidery, states, "in addition to enormous geographical diversity of costume, several distinct styles of festive dress and other garments co-existed in each village and each woman's collection at any one time, with richer women and villages possessing the greatest variety of garments and most lavishly ornamented."[2]

The styles have always changed as villages copied and influenced each other. Furthermore, with greater Western penetration in the twentieth century, the women copied patterns from European magazines, catalogs, and embroidery books that arrived in the region. Nevertheless, Palestinian women today, in many parts of the West Bank and among refugees, still have a strong sense of village identity and pride that "is expressed in specific designs and motifs, and in an aesthetic idiom (of embroidery)."[3]

Even after decades of dispersal, each person's origin in a particular Palestinian village or town remains an important part of their social identity, and this identity is often expressed by costume. Many women of village origin who have lived decades in refugee camps continue to make and wear traditional embroidered dresses like those who still live in their villages. During the last twenty years dresses embroidered in village style have become fashionable for evening wear among Palestinian city women living in the Arab countries, Europe and America.[4]

Fashion and style have never been stagnant. They changed and transformed with each generation as external and local influences, politics, and creative women introduced new ideas, motifs, threads, colors, fabrics, and so forth. Thus, the heritage of embroidery remains vibrant, lively, and expressive of contemporary Palestinian identity.

In addition, embroidery still has social significance because it indicates the marital status of a woman within her village or among the Bedouins. Unmarried women and younger girls wear modestly embroidered dresses, and the newly married wear dresses in vibrant colors with heavy embroidery, in accordance with village styles. Older women wear dresses that are less heavily embroidered with more muted colors. When in mourning or bereavement, the dresses and the embroidery are dyed deep blue. Frequently the embroidered chest panel was torn as a sign of grief, typically worn for the 40 days of mourning. The lavishness of embroidery varied also in terms of social class and status. Among the Palestinian Bedouins, young unmarried girls typically wore dresses with blue, often floral, embroidered designs; the newly married wore red embroidery; older women wore simple blue embroidery; and remarried women wore blue and red embroidery. The Bedouin women remain the only Palestinian women who cover much of their face with a triangular veil.

Fabrics

Fabrics were traditionally made of natural cotton or linen in Palestinian weaving centers such as Majdal, Bethlehem, Ramallah, Safad, Hebron, and others, whereas fancier silk and brocade fabrics and, during the Mandate period, velour, were imported from Syria. Some were woven with handlooms within the villages. Looser fabrics were preferred because they allowed for easier embroidering. Fabrics for dresses were typically dyed black or indigo, but in many locales, they were left undyed in natural colors. For example, Beit Dajan women often embroidered dresses on fabric that was left in natural colors. Velour was expensive and thus not worn in the villages but in the cities, especially Jerusalem.

Stitching and Patterns

Palestinian embroidery incorporates a variety of stitches. The most common in much of Palestine, especially central and southern regions, is the cross-stitch, also know as the village stitch. This stitch allows in particular geometric motifs and

Weaver at loom. © Steve Sabella/UNDP-PAPP

Woman in white *thobe*, walking past wall with graffiti. © E. Y. Farsakh

Black *thobe*. © E. Y. Farsakh

patterns to be embroidered, including eight-sided stars, triangles, chevrons, squares, and other evocative motifs such as cypress trees, palmettos, foliate patterns, flowers, peacocks, birds, and winged lions. A second popular stitch is the couching stitch, renowned in Bethlehem and the surrounding area, a striking stitch that allows ornate curvilinear, round, and floral designs. It is valued by the better-off social groups of the Bethlehem region and other parts of southern Palestine. What further distinguishes the embroidery of that area, particularly the villages of Beit Jala and Beit Sahur, is the use of metallic silver, gold, and silk threads that are couched into elaborate and ornate floral and curvilinear patterns and that are intricately filled with several other types of stitches. This was probably inspired in these Christian Palestinian villages by the ornate clerical robes and church furnishings that were traditionally decorated with silver and gold brocade and embroidery.

Another common stitch is the satin stitch, framed with couched thread and somewhat similar to the Bethlehem couching stitch. Other stitches include the *sabaleh* or herringbone stitch, used especially to join seams, for framing appliqué, and for embellishing and reinforcing hems, and the *habkeh* or binding stitch, which is used in a fashion similar to the herringbone stitch but typically for neck and sleeve openings. Finally, there are several other stitches that are used for joining seams, application of embroidered and fabric patches, and other purposes. Varied stitches often distinguish villages from each other.

Each region of Palestine had its own distinctive patterns or designs of embroidery, which were symbols of village or geographic identity and solidarity. Although social interaction, travel, intermarriage among villages, and a European presence influenced embroidery, certain design patterns remained exclusive to each geographic village grouping. For example, the palm tree, the eight-sided star, peacocks, and winged lions are still typical in the city of Ramallah; the amulet (for protection against the evil eye) is a typical symbol in the Jaffa region and among refugees; orange blossoms, the tree of life (signifying health), and rows of cypress trees are found in Beit Dajan; moon and feather motifs are common in Deir El-Balah; the Tent of the Pasha and other designs are typical of Al-Khalil (Hebron); the Pendent is a symbol of Gaza; the Cypress is often seen in Bir Es-Sabe' (Beersheba); and the couched floral and other curvilinear designs are common in Bethlehem. The most remarkable aspect of these designs is that many extend from Palestinian antiquity. Four-thousand-year-old dress designs found on Canaanite stone ruins show identical patterns to those still produced today.

Structure of Embroidery

Embroidery units are applied to the appropriate parts of a dress or costume in a distinct hierarchy, a symmetrical structure that follows a specific order of importance. First, the chest panel is embroidered, followed by the back panel, the side panels on the skirt, and, finally, the embroidery on the sleeves. Although the structure of the embroidery framework is common, it varies by the shape of its parts, in the internal arrangements to the parts, in certain exclusive patterns, and in the color shades by region and village. These styles were always changing as a result of the greater social intercourse among Palestinians and with Europeans. Thus, the width, number of panels, and other features of the embroidery on the skirt varied over generations in Ramallah. The so-called six-branch (panel) dresses of Ramallah recently became the standard among the West Bank villagers and refugee Palestinians in Jordan. Based on the structure, patterns, and colors of the embroidery, village and refugee women are able to identify the village or sub-region from which the dress or costume comes.

Color

Embroidery threads used until the 1930s were of natural dyed silk, principally from Syria. Natural dyes came from a variety of local plants and insects, including pomegranates, vines, plant roots (madder) for red, indigo for blue, cochineal, spices, and soil called *mugrah trop* for yellow. Since then, however, aniline chemical dyes of European perle cotton threads have become the standard since the 1930s and have been used extensively ever since. European threads are dyed chemically and have introduced an even greater variety and color subtlety to Palestinian embroidery. The color and shades of threads in embroidery also distinguished villages and regions of Palestine. For example, the Ramallah and Jaffa areas were known for the burgundy- or wine-colored thread. Gazans preferred magenta, and the people of Bir Es Sabe' were partial to scarlet and fuchsia. After the Palestinian Nakba,

the color language of Palestinian embroidery changed. On many dresses the dominant red was replaced by yellow, orange, green or blue, alone or combined and shaded threads (*muannas*) are popular in the 1980s. These changes were facilitated by the ready availability of a wide range of colours in perle cotton but, in view of the symbolic associations of embroidery color with regional and sexual identity, may have deeper significance.[5]

Variation by Region

Given all the elements that go into the production of embroidered dresses, costumes, jackets, head veils, and other accessories, variations abound among the regions and villages of Palestine, both in the pre-Nakba society and after. Starting in the north in Galilee, embroidery did not survive much into the twentieth century. Typical of the costumes in Galilee were long pants (*elbas*) and the embroidered long coat with short sleeves (*djillayeh*) worn over a white chemise (*qamis*). Galilee embroidery was renowned for the great variety of stitches used—the cross-, satin, hem, and stem stitches. The center of Galilee has always been Nazareth, the embroidery of which inspired many of the surrounding villages.

Oddly, the town of Nablus and the surrounding region has no tradition of embroidery, a fact that is not well understood. South of the Nablus region,

Ramallah, on the other hand, stands out for its needlework. Its famous fabric, known as *Roumi* was hand-loomed linen on which exquisite embroidery was sown. Beautiful, elaborate, and colorful geometric patterns were embroidered on off-white linen for summer and on black dyed linen for winter. With Western influence increasing in the area, Ramallah women began to embroider floral patterns on their white shawls and head veils. Ramallah and its surrounding villages have reproduced this tradition until the present. Indeed, after al-Nakba, Ramallah women activists organized one of the first women's cooperatives for the continued production of items of embroidery. In addition to dresses and costumes, this cooperative expanded the production of embroidery to the making of pillow casings, wall hangings, tablecloths, handbags, and other home decorations. Small, embroidered patches of cloth were framed inside cardstock and sold as greeting cards.

The Jaffa region was traditionally known for its fine embroidery. The stitches were small, the patterns intricate, and the garments elegant. The most famous and outstanding embroidery in this region was that of Beit Dajan. The workmanship and styles of Beit Dajan were of such exquisite style and quality that the village became famous for its fashions. Palestinian refugee women from Beit Dajan continue the tradition and produce dresses for markets in the West Bank, Jordan, and other diaspora communities that create a high demand for their workmanship.

Bethlehem continues to be unique among the Palestinian towns and villages producing embroidery because of the couching stitch and its use of silver and gold threads and elaborate patterns. Its wedding dresses are known as the *malak* or queenly costumes that brides proudly wear on their wedding days. No less desirable are the short *taqsirah* jackets.

Southeast of Bethlehem is Hebron, one of the oldest inhabited cities in the world. It has a rich cultural tradition not only in embroidery but also in hand-blown glass, ceramics, leather tanning, and weaving. The hand-loomed *qarawi* (village cotton fabric) was until recently woven in large quantities, dyed with indigo, and used for embroidering dresses and costumes. The women of Hebron principally used the cross-stitch and multicolored embroidery of various geometric designs, including stylized rows of cypress trees. Southwest of Bethlehem is the city of Gaza and its surrounding villages. The Gaza area is known for both its embroidery and its rugs. Its fabrics of cotton and linen are still embellished with imported silk stripes. Unique in the area of Gaza, especially Majdal and Isdoud, are dress patterns of alternating fabric stripes in green and red referred to as *Janna wa Nar* ("paradise and hell"). Refugee women from this area still produce such dresses in exile. Majdal was traditionally one of the greatest weaving centers, producing fabric for all of Palestine.

Among the nomadic tribal people of Palestine who were centered on the desert market town of Bir Es Sabe', the fabric was almost always dyed black; dresses were larger and more flowing than in other parts of Palestine. Tribal embroidery is also distinguished by the cross-stitch and emphasized embroidered panels, typically red with geometric patterns, on the lower front of the skirt. Here again, the status of the woman is typically announced through the color of the embroidery. As a bride or newly married wife, a woman decorates her dresses with varied shades of red embroidery. If widowed, she embroiders the dress or costume with dark blue embroidery. If she remarries, a woman decorates her dress with red, pink, and blue embroidery. Women from the Bir Es Sabe' area also embroider the head veil, face veil (among Bedouin women), and jackets, as well as cushions for their tent and home. Their embroidery also distinguishes the varied tribes of the area. Since al-Nakba, the Palestinian nomads have become sedentary or semi-sedentary but have largely kept a pastoral life and their unique traditions.

Contemporary Changes

Most Palestinian men today wear Western dress, but some, especially the working classes, also use the traditional *hatta* and *'egal*. Most Palestinian men thus are indistinguishable by dress from European and American men. Women's dress is somewhat more varied in the contemporary period. Particularly in the Gaza Strip, the rise of the Islamic sociopolitical movements in the late 1980s led many women to wear simple unembroidered long dresses with white unadorned head veils. Although this trend remains strong in Gaza, it is less so among the women of the West Bank, whose patterns of dress remain varied, and even less so among refugee women in the diaspora. These patterns are clearly subject to change and are a consequence of sociopolitical movements that are strong at certain times and wane at others. Most Palestinian women who live outside the refugee camps, particularly urban residents, typically wear European-style women's clothing.

TRADITIONAL AND CONTEMPORARY CUISINE

Palestinians and other eastern Arabs often say *Sahtayn* when a meal is finished. This expression means "two healths" to you. It embodies more than just a polite comment—it sums up the entire experience of eating in Palestine and the Arab World. Perhaps more than other cultures, Palestinians and other Arabs make an important social experience out of eating. In part it is because the offering of food is strongly incorporated into the values and customs of generosity and hospitality. Preparing, serving, and partaking of meals in family, among kin, and at other gatherings are the quintessential social activity among Palestinians of all social classes and locales. Although this happens daily on a smaller scale, it becomes particularly festive on special occasions, on weekends, and during the holidays.

There are dishes that are typically considered Palestinian, or prepared the "Palestinian way," but much Palestinian cuisine is familiar to many as eastern Mediterranean or Lebanese cuisine. It consists of common dishes, ingredients and spices used not only by the Palestinians but also by the Lebanese, Syrians, Jordanians, and, to some extent, the Egyptians. Perhaps with greater variation, the Greeks and the Turks also share much of this food. The Mediterranean diet is generally considered to be among the most naturally healthy diets in the world.

Bread and Rice

Bread is the staple of the Palestinian diet, with rice and bulgur wheat (*burghul*) a close second. Many dishes are vegetarian and rely on beans, legumes, and nuts. Olive oil is the main fat used in the Mediterranean diet, both in cooking and as a condiment. The making of bread is a large undertaking. It has been noted that "in the [Arab World], a [village] woman would set aside one day for making bread and bread dishes, which require the basic dough recipe, just as a day is set aside in the West to do the washing."[6] Although this was the traditional practice, today most families no longer bake their own bread but rely on bakeries. Daily or weekly treks to the bakery are made to purchase fresh bread, and it becomes a social outing and opportunity to visit and socialize with others. The general word for bread in Arabic is *khubz*. In the United States, this flat pocket bread is known as pita. Pita or *khubz* is used for sandwiches, dips, and as a base for meat, herb (*Za'atar*), or cheese "pizzas." The types of Arabic bread are varied, however. Beside *khubz*, rural Palestinians produce and use *Marqouq* or *Saj*, a very thin bread that is baked over a metal dome on an open fire. Bread of one form or another is

Baking bread. © E. Y. Farsakh

Ka'ak vendor. © E. Y. Farsakh

served at every meal, often with such popular side dishes as *hummus bi-tahini* (ground chick peas and sesame seed dip with spices and lemon juice) and *baba ghannouj* (mashed eggplant and sesame seed dip with spices and lemon juice). A small piece of bread formed as a little shovel between the fingers is often used in place of a fork or a spoon in eating a variety of side dishes and salads.

Rice dishes are also popular—combined with vegetables or meat stews or simply served alone. Many rice dishes are layered; some rice dishes are served with meat and vegetables such as cauliflower or eggplant at the bottom of the cooking pot, which is turned upside down when served at the table. These popular dishes are called *maqloubeh* ("upside down"). The preferred rice is long grain, and women consider it a source of pride to be able to cook rice that is fluffy, well separated, and dry.

Cheeses and Breakfast Food

Two Palestinian cities, Nablus and Akka, are famous for the cheeses they produce. The cheeses are known by the city names: *jibneh* (cheese) *Nabulsiyyeh* (of Nablus) and *jibneh Akkawiyyeh* (of Akka) are popular not only in Palestine but also in the surrounding regions. Both are made from goat's or sheep's milk, are white, and have the consistency of the hard cheddar produced in the United States. They are typically preserved in saltwater and have to be desalinated before eating, although some people like them to be somewhat salty. Breakfast food is typically comprised of *khubz* bread with these or other cheeses, including *labaneh*, a paste of soft cheese made from yogurt that has the whey drained from it. Those who can afford them also enjoy eggs. The breakfast table may include a variety of homemade jams and fruit preserves, and among the middle class, Western foods such as cereals as well. When the *jibneh Nabulsiyyeh* is placed in water for a long period of time, it is desalinated and becomes bland or "sweet," as it is called, and soft. It then becomes the base of a famous sweet desert called *knafi Nabulsiyyeh* (because the *knafi* of the city of Nablus is most famous) or simply *knafi*.

Soups and Salads

As in the West, soups are a favorite of many, especially in the winter months. Beans and other legumes (especially lentils) and vegetables are combined with myriad Arabic spices to give the soups unique flavorings. Many soups are made hearty by the addition of *burghul* or the addition of small meatballs.

Salads are many and varied due to the abundance of vegetables in the area. Some salads are most remarkable in their simplicity of ingredients such as the *salatat al-*

Carrying tomatoes. © E. Y. Farsakh

bandura (tomato salad) that requires only chopped tomatoes, cucumbers, and onions combined with garlic, salt, lemon juice, and olive oil. One salad in particular is considered a hallmark of Lebanese and Palestinian cuisine: *tabbouli*. It can be made with subtle variations, but it stands out because of the use of chopped parsley (normally used only as a garnish or seasoning in the West) and bulgur wheat. Tabbouli, along with *hummus* and *baba ghannouj*, have entered the cuisine of the United States and Western Europe and are sold prepared in many supermarkets.

Mazza

Mazza is the name given to an elaborate variety of appetizers comprising many hot and cold dishes; a small selection is served in homes before a meal or as side dishes, but very large selections are available at local restaurants. It is famous not only in Palestine but also in Lebanon and Syria. A version of it exists in Greece as well, as in Spain where it is called *tapas*. Some restaurants offer anywhere from 10 to 125 dishes of *mazza* and take pride in the variety, quantity, and quality of the offerings. Hot dishes include sausages, sautéed chicken, sheep kidneys, liver, spleen, and so on, as well as a variety of cheeses, fried vegetables, prepared pies, and salads. For the middle class, *mazza* is often the centerpiece of a family or group outing in the evening or over the weekend. The *mazza* and the meal are the basis of a social gathering that takes place over several hours of eating—actually nibbling—and socializing. It can be fun and very satisfying because everyone is able to sample many dishes and partake of the conversation and friendly gossip about family, politics, and world affairs.

Main Dishes: Meat, Fish, and Poultry

Meat prepared in many ways is the entrée of choice. Meat dishes are usually made with ground or chunks of lamb or beef. Chunked pieces can either be grilled on skewers with or without vegetables (called *kabab*) or served in stews. Meat may also be ground for use in a wide variety of dishes, one distinctive example of which is *kibbi*, a ground meat mixed with spices and burghul wheat and cooked in a variety of ways—fried, baked, or sometimes grilled. There is even an uncooked ground meat delicacy called *kibbi nayyi* (raw kibbi), a form of steak tartar with spices and burghul wheat. When there are large gatherings, the men of the family or village will oversee the preparation of the king of all dishes, a roasted, lamb, sometimes stuffed with a mixture of rice and spiced ground meat. Because of the Islamic prohibition and long historical traditions of the region, pork is not a part of the Palestinian cuisine. It has come to Palestine and the region from Europe, especially in the form of ham for sandwiches.

Because of the proximity of the Mediterranean Sea, fish is a popular entrée. Generally prepared fried, grilled, or baked, it is the sauces that make the fish dishes delightful. Fish is served with rice, salads, and other meatless dishes. The most popular sauce for fish is called *tarator*. It is made from sesame paste (*tahini*) and seasoned with lemon juice and spices. Shellfish is generally not a regular part of the Palestinian diet, although among the middle and upper classes, crabs from the area of Gaza are considered a delicacy.

Chicken is also used as the basis of main entrees. Grilled or baked chicken is a popular offering. At lunch and dinner, especially in large family gatherings, it is not uncommon for there to be meat, fish, and chicken dishes served.

Mahashi

Mahashi (singular form: *mahshi*) are a special category of dishes. Mahshi means "stuffed," and Palestinian cuisine is especially creative in these dishes. The stuffing can be either meatless (rice only) or with a mixture of rice and ground meat. The most *notable mahashi* are stuffed squash, including zucchini, and eggplant, grape leaves, and cabbage leaves. The *mahshi* considered by many to be the tastiest is *shaykh al-mahshi* (the sheikh of all mahshi)—very small, delicate eggplants (about one inch thick by three inches long) stuffed with cooked seasoned minced meat, pine nuts and other seasonings then baked to perfection. These dishes require a great deal of preparation, and it is generally considered an honor to a guest when *mahshi* is served.

Fast Foods

If there is any equivalent to American fast food in Palestine and the eastern Arab World, it is *shawurma* or gyro. It is probably a Greek or Lebanese innovation, but it is one that has become popular all over the Arab World and in locations in Europe and the United States. Often seen in open-air food stands or in the delis, these are large, cylindrical rotating skewers containing seasoned meat—lamb, chicken, beef, or a combination of lamb and beef. As the rotating meat is cooked, the preparer will slice off long, thin strips of meat that are then placed in *khubz* bread for sandwiches and served with vegetables, garlic paste, and pickled condiments.

Another popular food that is served as a meal or as a fast-food sandwich is *falafel*, a food originally from Egypt. Falafel is a deep-fried patty or ball made of ground fava beans (also called broad beans) or a mix of fava beans and chickpeas with special spices. Nowadays many Palestinians refer to the falafel balls or small patties as vegetable "nuggets" in imitation of the American chicken nuggets. The *shawurma* and *falafel* sandwiches sometimes have a *tahini* (ground sesame seed paste) sauce along with radishes, pickled turnips, and parsley, as favorite condiments.

Yogurt

A distinctive feature of the Palestinian cuisine is the use of yogurt (either from goat's or cow's milk). It is used in salads, as a dip, or as a condiment and also cooked in several delicious dishes. In salads, it is often combined with mint, garlic, and cucumber as a refreshing side dish. When used as a dip or as a condiment, it is usually made into *labaneh* (noted earlier), a paste that involves draining the whey from the yogurt so that it has the consistency of a soft cheese. When yogurt is cooked in a dish, it provides a "bite" that is complementary to other ingredients such as lamb, eggplant, or chickpeas. There is also an open-faced patty called a *sfiha* which is a small, square pizza-like appetizer that can be filled with *labaneh* and spiced ground meat or *labaneh* and tomato, which is unusual and tasty.

It is the sauces and spices used in Arabic cooking that make its dishes unique. Tahini, yogurt, and garlic sauces form the basic sauces for most dishes. Several vegetables are regularly pickled or preserved, as are candied fruits. Lemon, garlic, salt, pepper, and mint are the most common seasonings, with allspice, nutmeg, cumin, coriander, saffron, cinnamon, and sumac not far behind. Toasted pine nuts are regularly used as a tasty garnish as are toasted almonds in several dishes. Roasted nuts are often put out as appetizers or served with drinks prior to a dinner.

Sweets and Fruit

Arabic sweets are some of the most delightful in the world. Ground walnuts, pistachios, and pine nuts combined with honey or sugar syrup and phyllo dough

Knafi. © E. Y. Farsakh

make a layered pastry called *baqlawa* (similar but less gooey and more flaky than the Greek baklava). Other pastries are also made with nuts but instead of phyllo dough, they are either sandwiched between layers of shredded wheat or inside a cylinder of shredded wheat. Other pleasures included cookies, such as those with anise flavoring, and different variations of rice pudding. *Knafi bil-jibin* (also called *knafi Nabulsiyyeh*), a dessert made of unsalted soft cheese, like ricotta, covered with semolina flour and drenched in honey or syrup, is especially famous in the city of Nablus. Finally, *zalabi* or *luqmat al-qadi* is a deep-fried pastry, very light crisp doughnuts that are typically served during holidays. These two desserts are real treats.

Fresh fruit is regularly served at the end of meals either before or with dessert and is considered a mainstay of hospitality. The region has an abundance of fresh fruit to choose from in season, including fruit familiar to Westerners but also unique fruits such as fresh almonds, apricots, loquats, figs, dates, custard apples, and others.

Beverages

No meal is complete without a serving of Arabic (also called Turkish) coffee called *qahwi*. This term is probably the origin of the English word coffee because the beverage came to Europe via Ottoman Turkey as *kavah* or *kava* and then transliterated into coffee or café and other similar terms in European languages. *Qahwi* is made in a special coffee pot called *bakraj*, or *ibriq*, that is wider on the

Jalazon coffeeshop. © E. Y. Farsakh

bottom than it is on the top and has a long thin handle. The finely ground coffee often contains ground cardamom pods as flavoring. Coffee is measured into the pot along with the water (and sugar depending on the desired sweetness) and is brought to a rolling boil. Some connoisseurs bring it to boil up to six separate times. Coffee is typically served black and sweet during happy occasions such as weddings, holidays, and other celebrations, and bitter (unsweetened) during sad occasions; most times it is served *mazboutah* (just right) or *wasat* (medium) in sweetness.

Tea is a staple in the Middle East. It is served both sweetened and plain, and often with fresh mint. Coffee and tea are basic beverages offered on all social occasions. They are also served in offices and businesses, in many shops, in cafes, and in other gathering places. "White coffee" is sometimes offered as a digestive. This drink is made of boiling water with a few drops of orange blossom water or concentrate. It is very aromatic and flavorful and helps to settle the stomach, especially after a large meal. Sugar can be added to it according to taste.

Yogurt drinks are popular as are summer drinks called *sharab*, *shurbat*, or *sharabat*, which is a drink prepared with water flavored with sweet syrups made from varied fruit nectars such as pomegranate, mulberry, and others. Served on crushed or shaved ice, it evolved in the West as sherbet. Fresh juices are regularly enjoyed in season. Of course, Western soda drinks such as Coca-Cola, Pepsi, 7-Up, and others have also become popular. Alcoholic beverages are prohibited in Islam, but many secular Palestinians among the middle and upper classes, including the Christians, drink beer, wine, and other liquor. Wine has been produced in Pales-

Coffeeshop. © E. Y. Farsakh

tine since the nineteenth century. One local alcoholic drink, produced by the Palestinian Christians, is *arak*, a strong liquor made of distilled grape wine that is flavored with anise. Although a potent liquor, it tastes a bit like licorice. This liquor is also common to the Arab and non-Arab eastern Mediterranean countries. In Greece, it is called ouzo and in Turkey, *raki*.

The Social Aspects of Food

The women of the family consider the preparation of food a labor of love. The young girls and women of the family learn to cook at their mothers', aunts' and grandmothers' sides, beginning with the sharing of bits and pieces of recipes at a very early age. Measuring cups and spoons are rarely used. Often women of a family come to be known for their special dishes. When there are large gatherings in which everyone brings a dish, it is recognized that no one can do a certain dish better than so and so, and it would be unthinkable for someone else to prepare and bring it.

The preparation of food is an all-day endeavor. As soon as one meal is concluded, the preparation of the next begins. Breakfast may be simple, consisting of bread, cheese, *labaneh*, olives, tomatoes, and cucumbers, or it may be elaborate. Lunch is more elaborate and usually the main meal of the day. It is often followed by an afternoon rest. Dinner may be quite late at night. When there is a more formal meal (with the extended family or other invited guests), it usually follows a certain pattern. Because this meal has evolved into a major opportunity for socializing and fellowship with friends, neighbors, and family, it usually begins with the greeting of the guests. Children are required to be with the adults and to help serve. Everyone greets each new guest upon arrival and then sits in a circle in a room. Drinks are served (fresh juice or, if appropriate, alcoholic drinks) along with roasted nuts as appetizers. Often a *mazza* selection is offered.

Tables are filled to overflowing, and a meal is often served buffet style. It includes several main dishes of meat, chicken, and fish. There are also elaborate and numerous vegetable dishes, fresh salads, bread, rice, and, almost always, dips, olives, and pickled delicacies. The women usually insist that one sample every dish. One must go back for seconds, and, if they can convince you, even thirds. It is socially unacceptable to decline. Rather, one learns to take very small portions, so that one can gracefully go back for seconds with enough room to spare or to smile and say, "I will" and then just not go back. If it were a large party or a buffet where people are not paying attention to each other's food, a person would smile and say how wonderful everything is, even when he or she had not sampled it all. Social grace in these situations is elevated to high art and top-level diplomacy.

Following every meal are chocolates, Arabic sweets, a huge platter of all kinds of fresh seasonal fruit and the inevitable mint tea or the strong cardamom-flavored coffee. Unlike meals in the West, the socializing actually takes place prior to dinner and during dinner and dessert. Once coffee is served and everyone has finished drinking, it is generally known that this is the time to leave and everyone usually leaves more or less at the same time. This takes place especially if dinners are served late in the evening as is generally done.

If one wants to find the true soul of the Palestinian family, one need only join them for a meal.

NOTES

1. Shelagh Weir and Serene Shadid, *Palestinian Embroidery* (London: British Museum, 1988), p. 20.

2. Shelagh Weir, *Palestinian Costume* (London: British Museum Publications, 1989), p. 76.

3. Ibid., p. 104.

4. Weir and Shadid, *Palestinian Embroidery*, p. 14.

5. Weir, *Palestinian Costume*, p. 110.

6. See Madelain Farah, *Lebanese Cuisine* (Portland, OR: Author, 1972).

5
Religion and Religious Traditions

Palestine is holy to the three major monotheistic religions of the world: Judaism, Christianity, and Islam. For Judaism, it is the Promised Land; it is holy because the tomb of Abraham and the location of the first and second temples built during the ancient Israelite Kingdoms of David and Solomon. For Christians, Palestine is the birthplace (Bethlehem) of Jesus Christ, the town where he worked and lived before his mission (Nazareth) and the City (Jerusalem) where he was crucified, died, was buried, and then resurrected. Jerusalem also includes the Via Dolorosa, known in English as the Way of the Cross, which has not changed since that time. Jerusalem is the site of the Church of the Sepulchre, the site of the last supper, and the Garden of Gethsemane. The land and the cities of Palestine are saturated with the historic events and traditions that define Christianity. It is also the site of the founding Christian Church and earliest bishops of Christianity.

Jerusalem and Palestine are also sacred to Islam. Palestine is al-Ard al-Muqaddasah (the Holy Land). Jerusalem was the site of the overnight flight of the Prophet Muhammad to heaven and back. According to Islamic tradition, the prophet flew on a winged stallion (Al-Buraq) from a rock situated on the plateau in the city. Upon that rock, the famous Dome of the Rock Mosque was built in A.D. 691, not long after the death of the prophet. Jerusalem was the first of the two qiblas, the direction toward which the Muslims prostrate themselves when they pray. (Mecca is the second qibla and has become the permanent one for all Muslims.) Jerusalem is one of the three holy cities of Islam along with Mecca and Medina, which are in today's Saudi Arabia.

ISLAM AND PALESTINIAN MUSLIMS

Ever since the Islamic conquest of Palestine and the rest of geographic Syria in A.D. 638, Palestinian Muslims have had an unbroken physical presence and historical continuity in Palestine. The Arab presence in Palestine antedated considerably the arrival of Muslims, however. Following the arrival of Islam, Palestine was fully Arabized and extensively Islamized. Despite that, since the emergence of Christianity, the Christian Arab presence and continuity, as discussed later, has continued. Palestinian Muslims are part of a religious group that number more than 1.2 billion people today.

Since the Crusades of the Middle Ages, the Christian West has portrayed Islam and the Muslims in negative and hostile terms. The often deliberate and disapproving portrayal of Islam and its followers has received significant reinforcement since the colonial establishment of Israel on a large part of Palestine, and more recently with the attacks of September 11 on New York city and Washington, D.C. by a group of extremists claiming to act in the name of political Islam. Much of the negative portrayal and fear of Islam is in large part due to a misunderstanding of the religion and the behavior and interpretations of some of its practitioners.

For Muslims, Islam is the same truth that God has revealed to all his prophets, including Abraham, Moses, Jesus, and Muhammad. Muslims believe in one, unique, without equal God (*Allah* in Arabic). Indeed, the Qur'an (often spelled Koran in the West), the holy scriptures of Islam, repeatedly states that "Muhammad had not come to cancel the older religions, to contradict their prophets or to start a new faith. His message is the same as that of Abraham, Moses, David, Solomon or Jesus."[1] Mohammad never asked the Jews and Christians with whom he came in contact in the Arabian Peninsula to convert to Islam because they were peoples with holy revelations of their own. They were referred to in Arabic as *Ahl Al-Kitab*, the people of the Book (the Bible). The Qur'an states that there shall be no coercion in matters of faith. The faith preached by the Prophet Mohammad came to be called Islam, an Arabic word that means submission or surrender. A Muslim submits or surrenders his entire being to the will of God and to God's instructions on how to behave: individuals must treat each other with compassion, equality, and justice. Classically, for Muslims "the whole of life was potentially holy and had to be brought into the ambit of the divine. The aim was *Tawhid* (making one), the integration of the whole of life in a unified community, which would give Muslims intimations of the Unity which is God."[2] Mohammad did not have any formal education and was illiterate. Thus, the literary brilliance of the Qur'an was a miracle, the word of God revealed to Muhammad through the Archangel Gabriel. Muhammad recited these revelations to his followers. They were eventually recorded to become the holy scriptures of Islam, the Qur'an.

The Qur'an not only speaks of the oneness of God and the relations of human beings to God but also of the nature of the Islamic community or *ummah*. Social justice is a supreme virtue for the *ummah*. Muslims were commanded by God to build a compassionate and just community in which there is a fair distribution of wealth. For Muslims theological speculation was of less importance than the effort (*jihad*) to live the pious and ethical life according to God's law (*Shari'a Law*) that was detailed in the Qur'an, and interpreted as well in the *Hadith*, the record of the life, behavior and sayings of the Prophet Muhammad, the Perfect Man in Islamic tradition. According to one scholar,

In Islam, Muslims have looked for God in history. Their sacred scriptures, the Qur'an, gave them a historical mission. Their chief duty was to create a just community in which all members, even the most weak and vulnerable, were treated with absolute respect. The experience of building such a society and living in it would give them intimations of the divine, because they would be living in accordance with God's will.[3]

Contrary to some portrayals by Western media and some intellectual writings, Islam is a pacific faith. It has been noted that the "Qur'an does not sanctify warfare. It develops the notion of a just war of self-defence to protect decent values but condemns killing and aggression."[4]

Over the centuries, Muslims, like practitioners of other major monotheistic religions, developed their own rituals, shrines, sacred texts, doctrines, laws and legal schools, and mysticism: "Like Judaism, Islam is a religion that requires people to live a certain way, rather than to accept certain credal propositions. It stresses orthopraxy rather than orthodoxy."[5] For Muslims, there are five pillars, or principal obligations of practice to be observed. The first is the *Shahadah*, the declaration or profession of the faith that "there is no deity but God (Allah) and Muhammad is His Prophet." The first verse of the holy Qur'an states:

In the name of God (Allah), the most compassionate, most merciful.
Praise be to God, the cherisher and sustainer of the worlds
Show us the straight path
The way of those on whom Thou hast bestowed Thy Grace

This verse also starts the Muslim prayers, *Salat*, the second central pillar or obligatory practice of Islam. The pious Muslim is expected to pray five times a day at sun up, noon, the afternoon, as the sun sets and at night before retiring. Thus, five times a day, the *muazzin*, the religious cleric in the mosque who calls the faithful to prayer, chants:

God is great! God is great!
There is no (other) deity but God,
And Muhammad is his Prophet!
Come to prayer, come to success
Nothing deserves to be worshipped except God.

All over the cities, towns, and villages in Palestine and other Islamic countries, the people hear the *muazzin*'s call to prayer five times a day. In contemporary

Muslim women going to prayer. © E. Y. Farsakh

times, such a call cannot be missed because loudspeakers and amplification of the call from the minarets of the mosques resounds out all over the land. Before prayer, the Muslim is obligated to perform ritual purification. Prayer in words and action are performed in a ritualistic manner, facing Mecca. Prayer includes prostrating oneself before God. On Friday noon, the Muslim day of rest, congregational or communal prayer at Mosques, houses of worship, is usually performed. It is that communal prayer where a large number of individuals, side by side, pray and prostrate themselves together before God. This is often the only image of Muslims that is portrayed in the Western media. It is used to imply in a subtle manner the alien character of Islam.

Classically Islam frowned on the idea of religious clerics as intermediaries between man and God, but religious functionaries, including the *muazzin*, court judges (*qadis*), and religious scholars (*ulama*) emerged. A religious cleric, *shaykh*, manages the mosque, leads congregational prayer, delivers Friday sermons, tenders ethical advice, and officiates at Ramadan and other holy times. The *shaykh* presides and officiates over marriage ceremonies, divorce proceedings, and funerals. The *shaykh* also operates and teaches in the religious school, usually associated with the mosque.

The third pillar of Islam is *Sawm*, or fasting. Muslims fast during the holy month of Ramadan, the month that according to Muslim tradition is when the Prophet Muhammad received the revelations from Allah through the Archangel Gabriel. For Muslims, fasting from sun up to sun down is a monthlong ritual. During the daily fast, Muslims are not expected to eat, drink, smoke, ingest, or engage in sex or other pleasurable activities. Exempt from fasting are pregnant women, the sick, children, people traveling, and men at war. Fasting is a rigorous regimen and becomes especially difficult when the Ramadan falls during the summer. (The Muslim calendar, like the Jewish calendar, is lunar and thus the months cycle over the seasons, so Ramadan falls at different times of the year, rather than on a given day like many Western holidays.) Shortly after sunset, the fast ends, and family, neighbors, and friends gather to partake of a meal, called *iftar*, to break the fast. In the evening after breaking the fast, Muslims socialize, discussing family, community, national, and international affairs and reaffirming their values, customs, and traditions.

The fourth pillar of Islam is *Zakat*, or alms giving to the poor, indigent, and needy. Tradition dictates that Muslims offer a fixed amount (2.5 percent) of their income or capital to the poor each year. (In addition to *Zakat*, Muslims also give voluntary charity, called *sadaqah*.) From its start, the Islamic community was obligated to look after its needy through individual giving. This practice is especially common during the month of Ramadan when food is distributed to the poor. Over the centuries, alms giving and philanthropy became institutionalized. Property or capital given to religious institutions, including mosques, holy sites, religious schools, seminaries, hospitals, and orphanages, are not taxed. Religious property that may include urban real estate, agricultural land, or businesses, are called *waqf*. Thus, mosques and their associated institutions often become economically independent and are able to respond to the needs of the community. Palestine had a vast amount of *waqf* holdings. It was administered during the British Mandate by the chief religious cleric of the Muslim community, who was appointed by the Mandate authorities. Unlike the Catholic Church, however, such property is not centrally owned or controlled because there is no church or religious hierarchy. As with Judaism, Islam as an organized religion is decentralized; the religious clerics who manage and preach in the mosques do not answer to higher religious authority (like a bishop or pope in the Catholic tradition), but to the community. This varies in different Islamic countries, however. In some places, a ministry of religious affairs typically pays the salaries of the religious clerics.

The fifth pillar of Islam is the *Hajj*. The *Hajj* is the pilgrimage to Mecca during the twelfth month of the Islamic calendar at least once in one's lifetime. The poor who cannot afford to do so are not obligated. The annual *Hajj*, which began 1,400 years ago, is a universal congregation of Muslims from the four corners of the world and from all walks of life. It is unique both in action and scale. It brings together the faithful, not religious authorities, and has become a testimony to the universalism of the faith. The *Hajj* is a ritualistic experience that includes dressing in a simple white sheet fashioned into a robe. This reduces rich and poor, young and old, as well as different nationalities, to the same unadorned status. The pilgrims circle the *Ka'bah*, the central edifice in the Grand Mosque in Mecca, seven times, following the direction of the sun, and kiss the black meteorite stone, which has been embedded in the wall of the *Ka'bah* from time immemorial. The belief is that meteorite from the heavens links the site to the heavenly world. These rites can be performed at any time, but during the *Hajj* the pilgrims go from the steps of the *Ka'bah* through the nearby valley to *Al-Marwah*, where they pray. From there, they go to a flat plain called 'Arafat, where they stand in a vigil. They then visit a nearby site, *Al-Mina*, where tradition requires that the pilgrims throw pebbles in an act of stoning the devil. On the final day of the *Hajj*, they carry out an animal sacrifice.

Islamic Holidays

At the conclusion of the three days of the *Hajj*, the pilgrims and the rest of the Muslims celebrate Eid Al-Adha, the Feast of Sacrifice, in memoriam of the Prophet Abraham's willingness to sacrifice his son before God. On this occasion, Muslims typically slaughter a sheep, prepare it, and share it with others who are in need. This is a holiday that brings together family, clan, neighbors, and friends. Eid Al-Adha is one of the two most important celebrations in the Muslim faith.

The other is Eid Al-Fitr, the feast of breaking the fast. It takes place at the end of Ramadan, the month of fasting. It is one of the most festive occasions and also brings family and friends together in joy, celebration, gift giving, and other family activities. Eid Al-Fitr is preceded by a long month of fasting in which nightly celebrations associated with breaking the daylong fast also frequently involves gatherings of the extended family, friends, and neighbors. During this period, many people give to the poor: meals, sweets, some money, and invitations to share the *iftar* meals that break the fast.

PALESTINIAN CHRISTIANS

Many biblical and religious historical studies have noted, as others have said of Islam, that the Palestinian Christians have had a historical and continuous presence in Palestine since the establishment of the first Christian community in the times of Jesus Christ, 2,000 years ago.[6] Given the long and complex history of Palestine, especially its subjugation to external empires, foreign political or religious powers, and armies that have ravaged the land, Palestinians have never gained total or permanent control over their lands, resources, churches, or political institutions nor have they enjoyed political self-determination. Foreign domination has contributed to some Palestinian Christian migration in the past, but the Zionist-Israeli expulsion of Palestinian Arabs (both Christians and Muslims) in 1948 and the long and devastating Israeli occupation have caused the demise of the Palestinian Christian community.

The size of the Palestinian Christian community inside Israel, the West Bank, and the Gaza Strip has shrunk to near extinction. Whereas in 1948, the Palestinian Christian community constituted about 18 percent of the Palestinian population, it now comprises only about 2 percent of the West Bank and Gaza Strip population. The following is a brief review of the history of Palestinian Christians from the early founding of the community to the present and the contemporary Palestinian Christian groups (sects), their varied churches, theologies and rituals, and their church properties.

Palestinian Christians from the Time of Christ to the Coming of Islam

Palestine as a Roman province in the first century A.D. was far more diverse than traditionally conceptualized. It largely comprised Hebrews, pagan Greeks and Romans (particularly in Jerusalem, Caesarea, and Neapolis, which was later Arabized as Nablus), and Arabs in the southern hills and plains. As the birthplace of Christianity, many pilgrims from the known world of the day came, and many probably stayed. The Palestinian Christian community was small, poor, sometimes secretive, and fearful of Roman persecution during its first three centuries until the conversion and support of Emperor Constantine at the beginning of the third century A.D.

Roman persecution, especially in the second century, was also directed at the Jews of Palestine, who were prohibited from residing in Jerusalem. It has been noted that "from this point there appears to be no Jewish community living in Jerusalem. . . . Not to be overlooked is the fact that, while there was an interruption in the historical community in Jerusalem beginning in A.D. 135, there has been a continuous presence of the Palestinian (Christian) community from day of Pentecost until today."[7] Between this date and early fourth century, Palestine was largely pagan. In the middle of the third century, the Roman Emperor Decius launched a regime of systematic persecutions of Christians, especially those of Palestine, where many, including Bishop Alexander, were martyred.

Although destructive, it was not as severe as the Great Persecution under Emperor Diocletian (A.D. 301–303). This persecution was so severe that churches, sacred scriptures, and theological works in Palestine were all destroyed, Christians were expelled from public office and forced to worship Roman gods. They were often blamed for all the ills of the Empire and persecuted at the whim of local Roman officials.

In A.D. 313, Emperor Constantine issued the Edict of Milan, ending Christian persecution. Constantine moved the Roman capital to Byzantium, a tiny town on the Bosporus, straddling the narrow straight that separates Europe from Asia Minor. The great city that Constantine built at Byzantium was renamed Constantinople. During Constantine's reign and thereafter, the Christian community in Palestine and throughout the Empire flourished. There were three key features regarding the Christian community in Palestine during the three centuries before Islam emerged in the country.

The first was that, with the growth of the Christian population and imperial interest in Palestine, Christian churches were built and have survived until today. The principal two were the Basilica of the Holy Sepulcher in Jerusalem and of the Church of the Nativity in Bethlehem. The third oldest church in

Palestinian brothers taking a break from playing soccer. © E. Y. Farsakh

Palestine is Saint Porphyry in Gaza City, which also still stands today. Many other churches were built, including that of Saint Abraham in Hebron, probably on a site where a mosque has since been built. After the Israeli occupation, part of that mosque was turned into a synagogue. The second major feature was the growth of monasticism, the ascetic life and theology of monks who came from all over the Christian world of the times. By the early sixth century, more than 400 monasteries existed in Palestine within which 3,000 monks resided. These monasteries served not only the monks but also the rising number of pilgrims who came to the Holy Land from all the corners of the Roman Empire. With imperial attention and the growth of Christianity, Palestine flourished economically.

The third main feature of the period was the development among the leading Christian bishops of lively debates that set the theological basis of Christian orthodoxy in the region that is still dominant until today. Christianity in the region and in Palestine had one predominant church structure, the Greek (Byzantine) Church, but it included various other traditions: Nestorian, Armenian, Syriac, Latin, and Arab. All the sects and traditions lived in harmony in a pluralistic Palestine. By the end of the sixth century, Palestine was predominantly Christian, comprised of varied peoples including Arabs. The lingua franca of the times was principally Aramaic among the common people and Greek among the elite and ruling Byzantine class. In A.D. 638, with the capture of Jerusalem by Islamic Arab forces, the long tidal wave of change and transformation was set in motion in Palestine and the region. The process of Arabization and Islamization of Palestine started then. Palestine remained Arab and largely Muslim until the massive Zionist expulsion of its Muslim and Christian Arab population of the mid–twentieth century.

Palestinian Christians During the Islamic eras (A.D. 638–1920)

Symbolic of Islamic respect for Christianity and tolerance of Christians was the famous act of the Caliph Umar upon his triumphant entry into Jerusalem:

In Jerusalem, Patriarch Sophronius surrendered peacefully to the Caliph Umar when he handed over the keys to the city at the Church of the Holy Sepulchre. The Caliph refused to enter the great church and instead prostrated himself in prayer outside it, both as a sign of respect and to protect the church as his more zealous followers might have turned it into a mosque.[8]

In addition and perhaps more significant for the long run, Umar made a covenant to Sophronius, which gave the Christians of Jerusalem and the region full access and control over their holy sites and freedom of religion and worship under Islamic rule subject to payment of a poll tax. Furthermore, because Muslims were supposed to live in accordance with their religious laws, Muslim rulers allowed the Christian and Jewish sects of Palestine and the region to live by their religious laws as well, a tradition that survives until the present with regard to family law. The early Islamic period witnessed an interreligious dialogue between Christian and Muslim scholars, and by the eighth century, such a dialogue was conducted in Arabic, an indication of the success of the process of Arabization of Palestine and the region.

This religious harmony was undermined, however, as European Christian intervention was launched and led, at the end of the eleventh century, to nearly three centuries of religious conflict in the country and the region. This complex period brought conflict between Eastern (based in Byzantine Constantinople) and Western Latin (based in Rome) Christian traditions, the Muslim east and the Christian West (during the Crusades), and between competing Muslim regimes (Sunni based in Baghdad and Fatimid Shi'a based in Cairo). The Christian desire to recover Jerusalem and Palestine, first by the Byzantine emperors and later by the Catholic kingdoms of Western Europe and encouraged by the Pope in Rome, led to increasing native Christian and Muslim tension in Palestine. The most serious development began in A.D. 1096 when an official Papal Bull launched the First Crusade.

The Frankish Crusaders conquered Jerusalem shortly thereafter and slaughtered all Muslims, all Jews, and most Arab Christians in the city because they could not distinguish them on the basis of appearance, clothing, or language. The bloodletting at the hands of the Crusaders was horrendous, a fact that they themselves chronicled. To this day the Crusades are remembered as a legacy of the Europeans' savagery. In A.D. 1100, Baldwin, a leader of the European Crusaders, was enthroned as king of a feudal Crusader Kingdom of Jerusalem and much of Palestine. The native Christian Orthodox patriarch was expelled, and Western Latin Christian Catholicism was imposed on the city. Arab (Orthodox) Christians were banished from the city, and Arab Muslims and the tiny Jewish community were also denied residency in Latin Jerusalem throughout the period of the Crusades. Nevertheless, Palestinian Christians were allowed to practice their faith and their orthodox liturgical practices in the country outside the walls of the city. The Muslim Arabs, however, were killed, expelled, or enslaved by the Crusaders, while the small Jewish communities were reduced to nothing.

In 1187, Salah Ed-Deen (known as Saladin in Western historiography), ruler of Arab Muslim Egypt at the time, defeated the Crusaders who were led by King Richard the Lion Heart of England and liberated Jerusalem from the Crusaders. The Franks were expelled from Jerusalem, and the Orthodox Christian Palestinians were allowed to return and repossess their churches, receiving protection from the Muslims. Saladin also lifted the ban on the Jews living in Jerusalem, a ban that was imposed by the Romans in A.D. 135. Palestine after the death of Saladin was subject to invasions by outsiders for some time to come. For example, it was conquered by the Mongols in the thirteenth century and conquered again by the Egyptian Muslim Mamlukes (a slave dynasty), successors to Saladin's dynasty. It remained Arab—Muslim and Christian—under Mamluke and the successive Turkish Ottoman rule. The Palestinian Arab Christians reestablished their communities and reconstructed or repaired their churches; once again they were allowed to live by their laws under varied successive Muslim rulers.

Palestinian Christians under Ottoman Dominion

Arab Palestine, like the rest of the region, remained under Muslim Ottoman rule from 1517 until 1917. The Ottomans rationalized and politicized an administrative structure of the varied Christian (and Jewish) sects under their dominion. Labeled *Millets* (from the Arabic word *millah* for sect), the Ottoman authorities viewed the leaders of the varied sects as state functionaries. They represented not only their religiosectarian communities but were also responsible for collecting and delivering poll tax levies on their communities to the Ottoman Sultan. The Christian communities under Ottoman rule had a great deal of freedom and autonomy to run their religious and social affairs, administer their ecclesiastical family and personal status laws, and pursue any career short of high military and political positions.

Influence and control over the Christian holy sites, especially in Jerusalem, was contested between the Roman Catholic Church and the Orthodox Patriarchate in Constantinople. In the seventeenth century, France managed to negotiate with the Ottoman Sultan oversight of the holy sites for the Catholic Franciscan Friars Order, a sect that remains in place today. As the Ottoman Empire weakened in the nineteenth century, however, European state (political and economic) intervention and Western religious influence in Palestine and the region increased. As noted in Chapter 1, there was significant economic and political impact of that intervention on Palestine and the region. In addition, Catholic and then Protestant missionary and proselytizing activity had a profound impact on the Christian community in Palestine and the region.

Over three centuries of proselytizing, from the fifteenth to the eighteenth century, Catholic missionaries succeeded in splitting the eastern Orthodox churches and recruited factions and families to join or come into union with the Catholic Church of Rome. Known as the Uniate Churches, they adhered to Catholic doctrine and accepted the primacy of the Pope. These Uniate Churches, however, kept their Orthodox liturgy, some practices, and even some doctrines that differed from Roman Catholicism. For example, they used Greek and Arabic in their liturgy, not Latin. They also eschewed statues in their churches, although they have pictorial art and other icons. Today in Palestine, the most important of the Uniate Churches is the Greek Catholic (also known as the Melkite) Church, which split from the Greek Orthodox Church. A Greek Catholic seminary was established in the old Crusader Church of Saint Anne. By the end of the nineteenth century, the Catholics "had established throughout Palestine 30 orders, brotherhoods and associations, with 29 convents, 18 hospices, 6 higher schools, 16 orphanages, 4 industrials schools and 5 hospitals."[9]

Complicating this context was the fact that various Catholic orders including the Franciscans, Dominicans, and Carmelites, established educational institutions that taught their respective languages and created bilingual and multilingual Palestinian families, imbued to a certain extent with the respective European cultures, especially French and Italian. European Protestant missionary activity by British Anglicans, German (Prussian) Lutherans, and later Scottish and American Presbyterians and members of other Protestant denominations established religious, educational, social service, and philanthropic institutions in Palestine and the region. The Anglicans established an Ophthalmic Hospital and a hospice. By 1880, more than 100 schools and colleges had been established in the country.[10] The most famous is the American University of Beirut (AUB). First established in 1866 by the American Presbyterian mission as the Syrian Protestant College, it was based in Jerusalem. (After Lebanon became an independent state—created by France, the Mandatory Power—in 1922, the college was moved to Beirut and renamed AUB.) Like the Catholics, Protestant missionaries also recruited Orthodox Arab Christians into their churches and founded a number of independent Protestant denominations in Palestine. Most of the Protestant converts came from the poorer sectors of the Orthodox community. Although Roman Catholic converts had been increasing in number since the period of the Crusades, the Protestants gained only a small number of converts. In the twentieth century, evangelical Protestant denominations became active and managed to convert a smaller number of formerly Orthodox or Protestant Arab Christians.

All Euro-American missionary activity failed initially to convert the targeted Muslim Palestinians or the few Jews living in Palestine and thus shifted their efforts to the local Arab Christians. Nevertheless, the Christian church with the largest number of adherents in Palestine remains the Greek Orthodox followed by the Roman and the Greek Catholics. As a result of Catholic and Protestant missionary activity, the Orthodox churches in Palestine and the region were splintered and weakened. Thus, the Christian community in Palestine became fragmented into many churches and denominations and, except for the Greek Orthodox and Greek Catholic communities, became dependent on their European benefactors. Not to be completely outdone, pre-Communist Russia also established a presence in Palestine and set up religious institutions for Russian pilgrims in Jerusalem. The influence of the Russian Orthodox Church waned significantly after the Bolshevik Revolution. Most of the missionary schools and other institutions served the larger Palestinian population, not just people of the same denomination. Many Palestinian Muslim families, especially the middle class, sent their children to these Christian European missionary schools. The Muslim community in Palestine also became active in establishing educational, health, and social service institutions in the country, however. These Arabic-language institutions served the majority Muslims from all social classes.

In general, literacy increased in Palestine during the nineteenth century, and as printing presses were established, first by European missionaries and later by native Palestinians, it increased further. It also led to a literary renaissance and increased political consciousness. The Christian community of Palestine in particular became progressively urbanized and educated, engaging in contemporary occupations at a rate faster than their majority Muslim compatriots. From the nineteenth century, many of the Palestinian community and its political leaders—Muslim and Christian—emerged with an education provided by the missionary schools.

There were other important developments in the status of the Palestinian Christian Arabs in the late Ottoman era. European intervention in its varied forms encouraged Palestinian Christians to look westward for the first time. This, combined with the economic and political decline of the Ottoman Empire, led many to emigrate to Europe and the Americas. Palestinian communities in the United States, Chile, Colombia, and Honduras (in Central America) grew significantly over the years. By World War I, several thousand Palestinian Christians settled in varied parts of the United States. The total number of Christian Arab immigrants, including those from Palestine, to the New World may have reached 350,000 by the start of the war. Before 1914, Christian Arab immigrants to the United States and Latin America were known as "Syrians" or "Syrian Turks" because they arrived from the Syrian province, which included the district of Palestine, of the Turkish Ottoman Empire. By the last decade of the nineteenth century, emigration had led to a decline in the Palestinian Christian population in the Holy Land. By 1890 the Christian population in Palestine was 14 percent of the total. The population of Palestine at the time was 94 percent Arab (of which 82 percent was Muslim and about 18 percent Christian), 5 percent Jewish, and 1 percent foreign, mostly European.[11]

Palestinian Christians in the Twentieth Century

The ratio of Christians dropped further during the British Mandate period. As a result of migration and a lower birth rate, the ratio of the Christian Arab population declined to 9 percent by 1922. British Mandate authorities continued the Ottoman policy of religionational *millets*. Ecclesiastical courts were allowed to have jurisdiction over personal matters including marriage, divorce, adoption, alimony, guardianship, wills, and so forth and over the administration of church and mosque affairs and properties (*waqfs* or religious endowments). The Palestinian Nakba and the expulsion by Israel of about 750,000 Palestinians from their homeland in 1948 included about 50,000 Christian Arabs (about 35 percent of the total Christian population) who became refugees in the neighboring Arab countries. In 2000, the worldwide Palestinian Christian population was estimated to be roughly 500,000 of a total of nearly 8 million Palestinians—that is about 6.25 percent. Of these, about 65,000 live in the Occupied Territories and another 175,000 in Israel. The rest are refugees living all over the world, including in the Western Hemisphere. Of the total Arab population of the occupied territories of the West Bank and the Gaza Strip, the ratio of the Christian Palestinian population has dropped to just over 2 percent.

The Palestinian Christians continue to be divided into sects. Table 5.1 provides the contemporary ratios. The overwhelming majority of the Palestinian Christians in Palestine are Arabs but also include the non-Arab Armenian and Ethiopian minorities. The Syriacs are culturally Arab although they carry on the biblical tradition of using Aramaic (the language of Christ) in their liturgy. Despite their small population ratio, the Palestinian Christians, including the

Table 5.1
Approximate Distribution of Palestinian Christians by Sect

Sect	Percent
Greek Orthodox	52.6
Latins	30.0
Greek Catholics	6.0
Protestants	5.0
Syriacs	3.0
Armenians (non-Arab)	3.0
Copts	0.5
Ethiopians (non-Arab)	0.1
Maronites	0.2

Source: Data are from Bernard Sabella, "Socio-Economic Characteristics and the Challenges to Palestinian Christians in the Holy Land," in *Christians in the Holy Land*, ed. Michael Prior and William Taylor (London: World of Islam Festival Trust, 1994).

Armenians, have been active with their Muslim compatriots in resisting the Israeli occupation. They have leaders and activists not only in the political groups of the Palestinian diaspora but have also been active in grassroots resistance organizations in the West Bank and Gaza Strip during both Intifadas against Israeli occupation. One of the most unique acts of resistance in the first Intifada was a tax revolt in the Christian town of Beit Sahour near Jerusalem in the West Bank. This activism is the continuation of a long tradition—since the rise of Zionism as a threat to Palestine—of struggle by Christian and Muslim Palestinians in defense of their homeland and identity. It is a struggle that continues in the face of Israeli occupation of the West Bank and the Gaza Strip into the first decade of the twenty-first century.

NOTES

1. Karen Armstrong, *Islam, A Short History* (New York: Modern Library, 2000), p. 8.

2. Ibid., p. 15.

3. Ibid., p. xi.

4. Ibid., p. 32.

5. Ibid., p. 66.

6. This section is based largely on two works: Donald E. Wagner, *Dying in the Land of Promise: Palestine and Palestinian Christianity from Pentecost to 2000* (London: Melisende, 2001); and Michael Prior and William Taylor, eds., *Christians in the Holy Land* (London: World of Islam Festival Trust, 1994).

7. Wagner, *Dying in the Land of Promise*, p. 47.

8. Ibid., p. 61.

9. Anthony O'Mahony, "Church, State and the Christian Communities and the Holy Places of Palestine," in Prior and Taylor, *Christians in the Holy Land*, p. 18.

10. Ibid., p. 17.

11. Bernard Sabella, "A Century Apart: Palestinian Christians and Their Churches from Awakening to Nation Building," in Prior and Taylor, *Christians in the Holy Land*.

6

Literature

Palestinian literary and oral productivity shares with the rest of the Arab World a long and rich tradition. Because of the unique and tragic experience of the Palestinian people, however, many of the themes, issues, and content of their cultural production reflect their distinctiveness. A true Palestinian literature did not develop until the twentieth century, although its origins go back to the nineteenth century. What helped increase literary output beginning late in the nineteenth century was the expansion of education, especially as a result of missionary activity of the Western powers and Russia. Perhaps equally important was the introduction of the printing presses into the country, which encouraged the spread of education, readership, and literary and cultural interests. The development and growth of Palestinian print media encouraged the growth of prose writing. Essay writing became an important modern literary genre as well and became less traditional stylistically; writers addressed more directly political, social, and cultural concerns of the day.[1] Also, books on language, literary criticism, culture, religion, and politics were produced and avidly read before al-Nakbah.

The pioneering literary figures included Khalil Al-Sakakini (1878–1953) and Muhammad Is'af al-Nashashibi (1882–1948). Others, including Izzat Darwaza (1887–1984) and Khalil Baydas (1874–1949), advanced both essay and book genres and added translations of Russian and Western fiction as well. During the British Mandate, fiction writers appeared and developed the genre significantly. Among them were two pioneering and multitalented women who wrote poems, short stories, and novels: Samira Azzam (1925–1967) and Najwa Qa'war Farah (1923–). This chapter reviews and highlights a small selection of the literary output of the Palestinians, principally those literary contributions that were produced after al-Nakbah, because that event is the defining experience in modern Palestinian history and in the lives of its people.

Undoubtedly one of the greatest challenges that the Palestinians have faced in modern history has been how to tell their story. In a world where their history has become irrevocably entwined with that of Israel and often rewritten and distorted, it has become increasingly difficult for the Palestinians to make their voices heard above the highly volatile political discourses that surround the region. As the noted Paletinian intellectual Edward Said pointed out in a 1992 interview:

In the West Bank and Gaza, because people are so much in need of security, the Palestinians go from one day to the next and the last thing they want to do is to tell their story. They just want to survive. . . . Internationally, whenever a Palestinian tries to tell a story, to put in dramatic and realizable way the interrupted story of Palestine and its connection to the story of Israel, it's systematically attacked.[2]

Nevertheless, many Palestinians have overcome the odds to narrate brilliantly their poignant stories; some have made lasting contributions to the literary and folkloric world. Although only a few of the most prominent Palestinian literary figures are highlighted here, many others have significantly contributed to the rise of a distinct Palestinian voice in modern literature.

POETRY

Poetry, in both its written and oral forms, has been the principal product of Palestinian literary, popular and emotional expression for a long time. It is a literary genre that has the most defined character and tradition that date to pre-Islamic Arab oral epic poetry. Classical Arab fiction and drama were an important tradition, but their continuous evolution did not match that of poetry. Indeed, poetry is the favored genre of literary, romantic, critical, satirical, and political creation. In the contemporary period, poetry's lyrical rhythm and cadence continue and are often employed in romantic, nationalistic, and political songs. Of all creative writing among the Palestinians, and in the Arab World in general, more poetry collections are probably printed than any other genre. Modern Palestinian poetry is seen to be self-conscious, decidedly innovative, and often experimental in style, form, and content—all the more so now because of international literary influences.[3]

Oral Tradition: Folk Poetry

Palestinian oral folk poetry and song ranges from lullabies to political statements. They both are especially concerned with the subjects of love—yearning, lament, celebration—of a romantic sort, and of the family, friends, and country. The latter became all the more significant as the struggle against dispossession intensified and again after the catastrophe of 1948.[4] Contemporary folk poets continue to recite and sing of the heroes, martyrs, prisoners, and the national identity of the Palestinian struggle, including the Intifadas.

One of the he most popular forms of folk poetry is the *zajal*. In this form, two folk poets typically "compete in an impromptu debate in verse, thinking up their rhymed responses as listeners chant a refrain."[5] Humor, puns, and clever twists of the phrase are typical and especially appreciated by the audience. Traditionally, *zajal* poets were itinerant entertainers who traveled from one village to the other performing at weddings, celebrations, holidays, and other events. From those who retained them, they received gifts of food, cash, and occasionally other things. They recite their competing impromptu poetry with direct, relevant, and immediate personalized references to the occasion and the individuals involved and sing verses to the accompaniment of a *rababa,* a simple, one-stringed melodious instrument. With the advent of radio and television and recordings on cassettes, *zajal* poetry and poets are more popular than ever and are enjoyed by a wider audience.

Formal and Literary Poetry

Prior to al-Nakbah, poetry was common among Palestinian literary and intellectual figures. Its distinctiveness came about as a result of the threat felt by the Palestinian people to their homeland and subsequently because of al-Nakba. The poetry of the Palestinians has come to be popularly known as the "Poetry of Resistance." Although it has a unity of theme and focus, it has nevertheless developed varied structure, imagery, symbolism, and vision. Palestinian poetry created its own distinctive, self-conscious poetic form with its own themes, style, and imagery. It has been the emotional and expressive reaction to the collective national historical experience of the Palestinian people, from the threat of Zionism and al-Nakba to the destruction of their society and dispersal of most of the people. The efforts of powerful states, especially Israel but also Western and some Arab host states, to suppress Palestinian identity and nationhood has also contributed to the fierce sense of injustice and resistance in this poetry. Early resistance poetry expressed in identifiable images and symbols the communal and recognizable experience, reality, and shared hopes and aspirations of a dispossessed people. Much of the symbolic and metaphorical references derive from the Palestinian villagers' traditional involvement with the land, the foundation of their agricultural livelihood. Accordingly, the olive tree emerged as the most common symbol of Palestine and its people. In the sturdy and ancient olive tree of the Palestinian hills, poets see strength and endurance; in its roots, they see the tenacity of the history of the Palestinians. Poet Tawfiq Zayad (1932–1994) wrote:

Here we shall stay
Guarding the shadow of fig and olive trees.[6]

Resistance poetry had several distinctive features. The most noticeable is the tone of defiance, anger, rage and bitterness at the injustice that has befallen the Palestinian people—emotions that often have also been tempered by melancholy and sorrow. Heroism and tragedy also predominate. Yet personal issues of love and longing are never forgotten. Palestinian poets, like ancient pre-Islamic Arab poets, emerged to the Palestinians and their Arab supporters as national symbols, and their poetry as a mobilizing rhetoric and a language of resistance.[7] In pre-Islamic Arab culture, poets expressed their tribal identity, pride, and epic struggles in poetry. They were the spokespersons of their people. In the same manner, Palestinian poets have become spokespersons as they fashion their poetic creations into powerful aesthetic statements of national defiance and assertion.

Among the early Palestinian poets of resistance were Ibrahim Touqan (1917–1941), Abdul-Rahim Mahmoud (1913–1948), and Abudl-Karim Al-Karmi (1907–1980), better known by his pseudonym Abu Salma. Their poetry was modeled after the pre-Islamic traditional and classical Arabic form, *al-qasida*, or the epic poem. Perhaps it was their feeling of defense and preservation of their threatened Arab culture and traditions in Palestine that encouraged these pre-1948 poets to use the traditional form. The classical *qasida* can have as many as 130 lines, with each one ending in the same rhyme. It is "divided into two hemistichs . . . Furthermore, the form's monorhyme and monometer made it easy for millions of people to learn by heart and to chant at feasts, political rallies, strikes and even at the front. . . . It [was] direct, musical and impassioned."[8] During the great Palestinian rebellion of 1936 the *qasida* became a principal medium of inspiring and mobilizing the population of the country to resist British colonial control. Indeed, Palestinian *qasidas* of resistance often "crystallized political positions in telling lines which memorized by old and young, stiffened resistance and provided rallying slogans."[9] Many *qasidas* became powerful mobilizing tools for a people who were heavily illiterate and who were intuitively conscious of the threat to their homeland. Both Touqan and Mahmoud died by 1948, the latter in battle. Abu Salma went into exile in the United States. He lived and wrote in the Pittsburgh, Pennsylvania, area until his death in 1980.

Fadwa Touqan (1917–2003)

This tradition of resistance poetry was also strongly expressed in the work of the grande dame of Palestinian poetry: Fadwa Touqan, sister of Ibrahim Touqan, who died in early December 2003 at age 86. She wrote poetry as early as 1946. Fadwa Touqan published her initial collection, *My Brother Ibrahim* in 1946. Others— *Alone with the Days* (1952), *Give Us Love* (1960), and *Before the Closed Door* (1967) increased her stature. Her published poetry collections parallel and mark the evolution of Palestinian political consciousness since al-Nakba. Palestinian political consciousness evolved from the paralyzing feelings of shock, despair and the sense of being victims and developed into strong resistance and transformed pride and political elan.[10] Her poetic language always affirmed Palestinian identity. In a famous poem, "Call of the Land" (1954), Touqan tells the story of a refugee who feels pulled toward the sight of the former Palestinian city of Jaffa, lit up at night, and is compelled to cross the border into Israel, aware that he will die if he does so.

Fadwa Touqan's poetry links the traditional classical poets with the modern, and she depicted herself as a link in the chain of Palestinian history. In another famous poem, she asks nothing more than to die in her country, to have her body dissolve and become one with the grass and as soil to give life to a flower.

Touqan's poetry became distinctly more nationalistic in the wake of Israel's occupation of the West Bank, including her hometown of Nablus in 1967. In "Martyrs of the Intifada," a famous poem about the first Intifada of 1987–1993, Touqan depicted young stone throwers who faced Israeli tanks as having died standing on the road.

The tradition of the three male poets and Fadwa Touqan was picked up and elaborated by several Palestinians poets who had remained on their land after Israel was established. These poets included Tawfiq Zayyad, Samih Al-Qassem (1939–), Salem Jubran (1941–), and especially Mahmoud Darwish (1942–). The latter went into exile in 1970 and has become the uncontested poet laureate of the Palestinian people. Now world famous, Darwish's poetry has been translated into more than two dozen languages, including English. He has also won several international poetry and literature prizes, including the Lannan Foundation Prize for Cultural Freedom. Darwish is the best representative of resistance poetry among the Palestinians.

Mahmoud Darwish (1942–)

Mahmoud Darwish, the premier Palestinian poet, is probably the best-known and best-selling poet not only among the Palestinians but also in the Arab World. In a recent reading in Beirut, Lebanon, the audience reportedly numbered 25,000 people.[11] His books of poetry and prose have sold millions of copies all over the Arab world. He is also the best-selling poet in France[12] and indeed among the greatest poets of the twentieth century. Critics believe that Darwish is gifted with lyric intensity, epic breadth, and elegiac poignancy. He has lived through the devastation of war, the viciousness of politics, and the multiplicities of insecure exiles to produce powerful and eloquent poetry that is described as "a meticulous and spiritual excavation of land and language, diaspora and exile" while at the same time creating innovative excursions into new dimensions of poetry.[13]

Born in 1942 in al-Birweh, a small village in the Galilee region of Palestine, Darwish became a refugee at age six following al-Nakba. His family spent a year in a refugee camp in neighboring Lebanon and then, like many Palestinians, returned "illegally" in 1949 to what had become Israel, but found al-Birweh was one of at least 400 Palestinian villages razed by Israel and depopulated of Palestinian Arabs, with Jewish colonies built on their ruins. Darwish said, "We lived again as refugees, this time in our own country. It's a collective experience. This wound I'll never forget."[14] He and his family missed the very first census of Palestinians in Israel and therefore were labeled by Israel as "present absentees," a strange and unprecedented legal category that denied them citizenship and most other rights. In short, they became refugees in their homeland.

For Darwish, Palestine is a metaphor for the loss of an earthly paradise, for birth, death, and resurrection, and for the anguish of dispossession, destitution, and exile.[15] Palestine is the earthly paradise that has been lost twice.[16] The intensity of Darwish's poetic evocation of what has been lost has produced in his Palestinian readers their own memories of their lost homeland. Using ancient or traditional fable, folktale, myth, legend, or epic in the imagery and symbolism of his poetry, Darwish captivates his readers with both the eloquence of his style and the evocation of subtle meanings.[17] The natural, mythical, and spiritual symbols in his poetry, such as rock, mountains, trees, and the sea, are indigenous and therefore evoke Palestine.

Darwish's development as a poet has been seen to have proceeded in several stages. In the first, the lyrical stage, Darwish spoke of his personal experience as representative of the experience of his people. He drew on those experiences in his early poetry. At age 22, he electrified the Palestinian and Arab world with the poem "Identity Card," a forceful and dramatic monologue, recounts a run-in with an Israeli police officer who had stopped Darwish to check his papers. This poem was one of the most compelling examples of the affirmation of Palestinian Arab identity, pride, defiance (of Israeli control), and of the spirit of resistance. It launched Darwish as the Palestinian poet par excellence. This and subsequent stages of Darwish's poetry use style and imagery evocative of Palestine and the memory and struggles of its people. For him, as for all Palestinian poets, such a struggle is existential.

The second stage evolved beyond the direct and forceful rhetoric of declamation to a less direct, subtle, and more eloquent style. It was the period of "the dreaming revolutionary," as he describes it.[18] The subsequent stages are those of the mature Darwish, whose poetic craft is honed and more innovative and whose style more elegant. As one critic notes, "His sense of cadence is symphonically structured, and has few equivalents among modern American poets."[19] The musicality of Darwish's poetry is further affirmed by the resonance of his reading.[20] In the third stage, Darwish takes on universal themes that are more introspective and consummately sophisticated. He is a poet "who transforms astronomical expanses of human emotions into the clear crystal of poetry."[21]

The New Palestinian Poetry

Although contemporary Palestinian poetry continues to be nationalistic, it nevertheless exhibits much greater diversity in expression and sophistication of poetic technique. New concerns in form and content, in the use and evocation of symbols, imagery, and figurative language have emerged. The characteristics of the newer Palestinian poetry lie in the use of archetype and myth, biblical allegory, self-criticism, and language.[22] Regarding the latter two aspects, Ali al-Khalili's poetry, especially his poem titled "What Is Your Purpose, Murderous Beauty," is exemplary. The poem "exemplifies a conscious aesthetic-linguistic revolution which is inseparable from the socio-political revolution that the poets are calling for."[23]

FICTION

Contemporary Palestinian fiction derives in large measure from the native oral tradition of folk tales and storytelling and the classical Arab literary fictional narrative. The latter included the magnificent *Thousand and One Nights* (often referred to as *Arabian Nights*), an episodic or serial story told over that number of nights; *al-Sira*, ("biography"); the medieval romantic stories such as *Majnoun Laila* and *Qais wa Lubna;* and the imaginative animal fables such as *Kalila wa Dimna*. Palestinian fiction is inspired both by the rich legacy of the past and the dynamic forms, styles, and content of global literature.

Palestinian fiction was produced in various contexts in the locations where writers found themselves after al-Nakba: in the diaspora, inside Israel, and under occupation after 1967. The varied experiences and environments had a profound influence on the content, form, and style of the fiction they produced. Ghassan Kanafani, Jabra Ibrahim Jabra, and Samira Azzam wrote in the diaspora, whereas Emile Habibi, Tawfiq Fayyad, Hanna Ibrahim, Antone Shammas, and others produced fiction inside Israel. Before 1967, Majed Abu-Sharar, Yahya Yakhlef, and others in the West Bank were joined by Gazans such as Zein al-Abideen al-Husseini, Fawzi al-Umari, and others who produced a variety of narrative literature. In general, the Palestinian narrative literature after al-Nakba and before 1967 was sentimental and tinged with sorrow and even self-pity as a result of the tragedy that had befallen the country and its people. Soon after the Israeli occupation of the West Bank and Gaza and the rise of the Palestinian resistance movement, the character of the narrative transformed significantly in all respects—structure, content, and form.

The Short Story

The short story became the most popular form of Palestinian fiction. The genre is open and receptive to "the devices of other artistic forms, such as film . . . romance, fable, parable, folk tale, etc. (and) have resulted in a dynamic and multifarious movement which continues to be experimental and innovative."[24] Like poets, fiction writers have also experimented with language, abandoning the classical forms and relying more on a colloquial voice, responding to the fact that most of Palestinian society are peasants or of peasant origin. Despite all the experimentation, the reality of the Palestinian people continues to provide a unifying theme for all writers of fiction. Folk motifs and contexts continue to be dominant. Yet this fiction addresses itself especially to the Palestinian people as a vehicle to conceptualize and mobilize for change. It is politically engaged and not neutral, a conscious creative and aesthetic construction committed to the cause of its people, an important example of what has come to be called "committed literature."[25] In such works, the peasant or common person is often a symbolic or allegorical character representing the Palestinian people as a whole.

A good example of short story writing that innovatively combines folk and classical tradition in style, form and content is Zaki Darwish's "A Thousand and Two Nights." The story is composed of five episodes. Although it follows the original model, Zaki Darwish's story uses allegory for literary and political ends. Indeed, it condemns a society that has "fallen victim to its own fantasies of the past and neglected the demands of the present and the future."[26]

Another example of the Palestinian short story is that of Mahmoud Shuqeir. His story "The Man Who Rose from the Living" is in the form of a biblical parable. The main character is a martyr and a redeemer, "the archetype of Palestinian resistance, *feda'yeen* (those who sacrifice) . . . whose patient suffering, is the life-giving redemptive force."[27] Other innovative short story writers include Emile Habibi, Muhammad Ali Taha, Muhammad Ayyoub, Ibrahim al-Zant (who writes under the pseudonym of Gharib Asqalani), Akram Haniyya, and others.

The Novel and Novelists

The novel is a relatively new concept to Palestinian artistic expression, but it has become vastly popular in recent times. One reason for this is that the novel allows authors to describe their situation and surroundings specifically, freeing them from poetic bonds that are better used to depict emotion than action. For the Palestinians, then, the novel has become an useful way of conveying the truth about their lives under Israeli occupation. It has also become a useful tool for Palestinian feminist writers, who have learned to make their voices heard and encourage social justice through the telling of their stories. Poet Mahmoud Darwish recognized the increased utility of the Palestinian novel in reflecting a genuine Palestinian reality: "the poet was once everything to Arab culture: journalist, professor, leader. . . . The form to which I most aspire to fulfill now is the novel. There is no one in this age that I envy more than the novelists because the novel can expand to include everything. . . . In the novel you can sing, and speak poetry, prose, ideas, and practically everything."[28]

Therefore, the Palestinian novel has taken on a new dimension in recent times, becoming a primary vehicle for expressing the reality of a life lived under occupation. The Palestinian writers who have emerged from this experience have created some of the most original and rich contemporary novels, blending the emotional depth of their poetry with the powerful storytelling capabilities of the modern novel. Themes such as identity, political impotency, and nationality are prevalent in contemporary Palestinian literature. Inevitably, the experience inside Israel, the loss of the homeland, the effects of the diaspora and the long occupation play major roles in any fictional (or nonfictional) description of Palestinian reality. In essence, the Palestinian novel seems to have become an autobiographical tool that various authors have employed to reflect their own feelings of alienation or helplessness. It has also become a venue for suggesting answers to individual and social dilemmas. Transcendence, redemption and spiritual revolution are usually offered at the climax of most novels, when the characters are able to find an existential identity for themselves. The connection between the lost identity of Palestine and the loss of a sense of self are often paralleled in novels, such that the very essence of the protagonist becomes entwined with the history and the land itself, regardless of where the actual story takes place.

The Palestinian novel has yet to encompass fully the reality of common Palestinian life. As a relatively new genre of expression, it is still in its adolescence but promises to fill a void once it reaches its potential. Any Western lover of fiction will find the Palestinian novel to be an enriching, and oftentimes refreshing, divergence from the Western ideal. The poetic nature of the novels, combined with the originality of their structure, typically carries the reader on an aesthetic trip through the history, emotions, and struggle of the Palestinian people. In a way then, the novel has become an effective mechanism to tell the true story of the Palestinians whose everyday life extends far beyond the perpetual images of struggle and conflict that are broadcast to the West through the media. The novelists are many. Following are some of the most prominent and samples of their works.

Sahar Khalifeh (1941–)

The rise of Palestinian literary popularity has been accompanied by the development of a distinctly feminist voice in Palestinian novels. A string of prominent writers have emerged to tell women's stories of loss and alienation that have accompanied Israeli occupation, and premier among these writers is Sahar Khalifeh.

Khalifeh was no stranger to the harsh nature of foreign occupation. She was born and raised in a middle-class family in the West Bank town of Nablus, which was under a British Mandate at the time of her birth in 1941. She completed her secondary education at Rosary College in Amman at the age of 18 but discontinued her studies when she married. Thirteen years later, her divorce freed her to return to her educational goals, and she enrolled at Bir Zeit University in the West Bank, where she obtained a bachelor's degree in English literature. Then, thanks to a Fulbright grant, she was able to continue her studies at the University of North Carolina and the University of Iowa, where she eventually received a Ph.D. in women's studies and American literature in 1988. Her nonliterary accomplishments included various professorial positions and founding the Women's Affairs Center in Nablus that has expanded to several other cities.

In her dissertation, Sahar Khalifeh describes the situations in her youth that led her to become an ardent feminist and a writer. She refers to the gloom surrounding her birth, as the fourth girl in a family with no male heir: "In that gloomy and unfriendly atmosphere I learned my worth in this world. I learned that I was a member of the useless, helpless, unredeemable sex. I was told from childhood on to prepare myself for the consequences of being a woman. I was told that I had to learn how to obey orders and submit to rules which covered every detail of my life. . . . As a means of escape I resorted to reading, writing, and painting."[29] She also details the events surrounding the abandonment of her father, who left the family for a new, younger wife after the male heir who had finally been born was crippled in a car accident at age 16.

She speaks of her sense of defeat after the 1967 war, when she began to realize that "our political defeat was a reflection and a natural result of our cultural one. It made me see clearly the final fruits of our sick values. Defeated individuals cannot win a war against external forces. To win the war, we would have to start with our internal sicknesses . . . have to re-evaluate our social values, our social structure, family system, educational system, and the impact of all of those on the citizen from birth until death."[30] This experience led her to writing, and after her first novel was accepted for publication, she left her abusive, arranged marriage to begin her life anew.

Her first novel, *We Are Not Your Slave Girls Anymore,* was published in 1974 but was confiscated by the Israeli occupation authorities. It had a broad impact because of its strong feminist theme. Dealing with the educated class of Palestinian society in the Jordanian controlled West Bank of the pre-1967, the novel was remarkable for its frequent use of colloquialisms and intense dialogue. In fact, Khalifeh is one of the first Palestinian writers to invoke common dialogue in her works. She explained the reasoning behind this in an interview, during which she asked, "Can you imagine for example Khadra, an ordinary woman from the slums in Nablus speaking in classical Arabic, or the intellectual speaking in the same language as Khadra? We live in a society with different people, and these people speak in a different manner. . . . The language of the street is simple and crude, and this is what I seek to convey."[31] Apparently the public agreed with her, because the novel was popular enough that it was turned into a television series and radio program.

Her second novel, which came out in 1975, became her most acclaimed novel. In *Wild Thorns,* Khalifeh examines the nature of the migrant Palestinian labor force in Israel and the internal effects this labor has on Palestinian society. The novel addresses the internal discourse within Palestinian society that brands the workers from the Occupied Territories who have ventured into Israel to make their living as traitors. The story revolves around four main characters, each of whom must struggle with the reality of the Israeli occupation. One of the characters, Usamah, returns to Palestine after five years with the idea that he will blow up a bus carrying these "traitorous" workers into Palestine to deter economic collaboration. His plan goes awry when he finds out that his intended comrade and cousin has actually been forced to become an Israeli worker himself to pay for the medical treatments that are keeping his dying father alive. The novel revolves around these similar men who have had a very different response to the Israeli challenge. Unlike her first novel, there is no female protagonist in *Wild Thorns.* The international acclaim that has surrounded the novel has led to its translation into many languages, including English.

Khalifeh's other major works include *The Sunflower* (1980), in which the youngest of the main characters in *Wild Thorns*, Basil, reappears from his prison term. *Sunflower* actually is an independent self-contained sequel to an earlier novel, *Al-Subbar*. *Al-Subbar* itself is a very interesting rendition of the political factions and movements resisting Israeli occupation. *Sunflower*, is a dramatic and realistic representation or depiction of the actual complex reality of Palestinian life, whether under Israeli occupation; in the city, suburb or village; or in a refugee camp. The novel emerges as a sensitive novelist's call not only for freedom from an authoritarian and brutal occupation but also from the bondage of oppressive traditions.

Khalifeh's *Memoirs of an Unrealistic Woman* (1986) has an autobiographical element in its examination of a woman caught in a loveless marriage; two other books are *The Door of the Courtyard* (1990) and *The Inheritance* (1997). As the most widely translated Palestinian author next to Mahmoud Darwish, her novels are a must read for anyone interested in Palestinian literature. She currently lives in Nablus where she continues to write and promote issues of public concern to the Palestinian community. Her most recent endeavor has been to produce a television series she says is intended to "entertain through covering subjects of development that effect our society, such as hygiene, values and traditions, health of women and children."[32]

Ghassan Kanafani (1936–1972)

Ghassan Kanafani is another prominent Palestinian writer whose work has taken many forms. As a journalist, short story writer, and novelist, Kanafani beautifully captures the essence of the Palestinian struggle for identity in many of his works. He was born in Akka (Acre) into a middle-class family in 1936, the year that marked the start of the Palestinian revolt against the British Mandate. His primary education was at a French-language missionary school, but at age 12 his family was forced from their home. They became refugees in Syria, where his father struggled to find employment. Kanafani discontinued his francophone education and eventually studied Arabic literature at the University of Damascus. During these years, he embarked on a teaching career with the UNRWA schools in Palestinian refugee camps, but his political affiliations led to his expulsion from the university and exile to Kuwait. Five years later, he moved to Beirut, where he became a leading member in the Popular Front for the Liberation of Palestine, one of the main Palestinian political factions, and editor of *al-Hadaf* ("The Goal"), its weekly magazine. He remained there, active in the pro-Nasserist, Arab nationalist movement until his assassination in 1972 by a car bomb planted in his car by Israeli assassins. His young niece was also killed in the explosion.

Kanafani's major works usually revolve around the theme of refugee life and the trauma of losing one's homeland. His journalistic legacy is extensive, but he also published 11 books before his life was cut short by the Israeli assassination.

The most famous novel he wrote, *Men in the Sun* (1962), follows three Palestinian refugees in their struggle to smuggle themselves from Lebanon to Kuwait to seek employment. They encounter innumerable obstacles as their present situation is explained through flashbacks; their story culminates in tragedy when a hot day and unexpected delays throw their plans awry. At the Kuwait border, they suffocate and die from the heat while hiding inside the hull of an empty tanker in which they were to be smuggled into the country. This story is emblematic of the struggle of displaced and dispossessed Palestinians trying to make a living in a hostile social and political environment even among their Arab brethren.

His second novel, *All That's Left to You* (1966) also received considerable attention in academic circles. It deals primarily with a brother and sister who each fight their respective battles, one against Israeli occupation and the other against an abusive husband. He also wrote *Land of Sad Oranges* (1962), *Return to Haifa* (1967), and *Umm Sa'd* (1969), among others. Throughout his later work, there is a definite Marxist theme; many literary critics felt his ideological intensity compromised his work. *Men in the Sun* and *All That's Left to You* are nevertheless remarkable novels.

Jabra Ibrahim Jabra (1920–1994)

Born in 1920 in Bethlehem to a Christian family, Jabra Ibrahim Jabra rose to become one of Palestine's most prominent novelists. His poverty-stricken childhood forced him to work as a carpenter and plumber while attending school after his father was permanently disabled by severe rheumatism. He was nonetheless able to continue his schooling, eventually attending Cambridge University in England. With his English skills, he was able to return to Palestine to teach English at various schools and colleges until he and his family were driven from their home by Israeli forces in 1948. Jabra then sought refuge in Iraq, where he later became a citizen and continued his work as an English teacher and professor. Later in his career, he worked for the Iraqi National Oil Company, lectured throughout Europe, converted to Islam, and studied literary criticism at Harvard University. He died in 1994. In addition to the novels he wrote, Jabra was also a preeminent literary critic who penned several collections of criticism on contemporary Arabic poetry and was himself a poet. He translated many English novels into Arabic and produced many paintings.

In his own works, Jabra was consistently concerned with pan-Arab ideals and Arab cultural heritage. He was influenced by both Arab and Western literary tradition, having an extensive knowledge of both through his studies. He frequently expressed his desire to fuse his knowledge of these two very different traditions to enrich the content, appeal, and versatility of Arab literature, and his writings were widely acclaimed. His novels often address themes of the revival of Arab society, the struggle of the displaced Palestinian immigrant, romantic love, and female promiscuity. Interestingly, some have criticized his work as pornographic and misogynistic.

Perhaps his most significant contribution to the Palestinian and Arab novel is his use of various literary techniques. As one critic notes, Jabra constantly experimented with literary devices that best suited his creative themes, inspired by both Arabic and Western narrative traditions. Jabra "has skillfully employed a wide range of techniques: stream of consciousness, interior monologue, multipresentation, and fragmentation of time."[33] The Western influence and a perceived intellectual elitism in his work have, however, garnered negative criticism. Nevertheless, his two primary Arabic novels, *The Ship* (1973) and *The Search for Walid Masoud* (1978), both of which can be found in English translations, are highly involved, introspective, and regarded.[34]

Jabra's contribution to the evolution and structure of the Palestinian and Arab novel and the influence of Western literary tradition can be clearly seen in *The Ship*, which is reminiscent of the works of the American novelist William Faulkner. In it the characters find themselves aboard a ship sailing from Beirut to Naples. The main character, Isam Salman, is trying to escape the pain of his lost love, Luma, whom he could not marry because of an old tribal feud that began when his father killed her uncle. Consequently, she marries his friend, an Iraqi doctor named Falih Haseeb. The novel's central conflict takes place when Luma decides to try and renew her love affair with Isam by convincing her husband to take the same cruise. Little does she know that her husband only accepts because he, too, has a lost love, who will also be on the cruise. The love circle in the novel revolves around a man named Wadi', who fought and lost his best friend in al-Nakba. His girlfriend is forced to leave him alone on the cruise to attend a conference, but returns to him later in the trip, deciding to skip the conference in deference to her love for him. In her absence, he meets an intriguing French woman. A wrench is thrown into the story when Haseeb commits suicide. Through these complex relationships the novel explores the nature of love and loss, the tragedy of al-Nakba, and the artistic revival of Arab society. The connection between the history of the characters and their present decisions is beautifully interwoven by the reflections of the two main narrators, Wadi' and Isam.

Most of the literary criticism written about Jabra's work is based on *The Search for Walid Masoud*. This novel begins with Masoud found to be missing from his home in Baghdad. His car was abandoned at the Syrian-Iraqi border with a revealing tape stashed inside. A group of characters who have known Walid in various capacities meet in Baghdad to listen to the tape in an attempt to unravel the mystery surrounding his disappearance. What they find surprises them, as the garbled tape reveals aspects of his character of which they had been unaware. This leads them to come up with their own explanation for his disappearance, each explanation differing radically from the next, reflecting the importance of perspective when dealing with a single character. Little effort to find Walid is made, but the various characters paint, through their memories of the man, a vivid portrayal of him. The novel ends ambiguously, never clearly revealing what became of Walid, but it does insinuate that he may have returned to Palestine to fight for its liberation.

Walid Masoud in some respects represents an attempt to depict an autobiographical character. Walid is a heroic warrior, devoted to his homeland, with a magnetic appeal to women. He also shares many experiences and ideas with Jabra. Like Jabra, he is an intellectual who is driven from his home to live in Baghdad after al-Nakba. This novel also reflects Jabra's intense commitment to bring the Arab World into his view of modernity. The characters experience a sense of loss—not only of Walid, but of themselves. They seek to reconcile their sense of self with their new reality. The novel is another must read for anyone interested in Palestinian literature.

Jabra's second novel, *Hunters in a Narrow Street* (first published in English in 1960), perhaps also autobiographical, deals primarily with a Palestinian Christian intellectual, Jameel Farran, who becomes a refugee after the Palestinian and Arab military defeat and al-Nakba. The novel tracks his journey from Bethlehem to Baghdad, where he becomes an English teacher.

Emile Habibi (1921–1996)

Like Jabra, Emile Habibi was born into an impoverished Christian Palestinian family under the British Mandate. He was exposed at an early age to communist ideals when his home in Haifa became a meeting place for the Palestine Communist Party. This influence had an enduring effect on Habibi, who would later become an ardent supporter of communism and the Soviet experiment until its disintegration in 1991. Even during the British Mandate years, Habibi led the Communist Party in its underground activity. Unlike the rest of his family who became refugees in the Palestinian diaspora after al-Nakba, Habibi chose to stay in what became Israel and become a citizen. From 1952 until 1972, he served as the representative of the Communist Party of Israel (CPI) to the Israeli Parliament, the Knesset. He even established and edited the newspaper for the party, becoming one of the primary Arab spokesmen for the Palestinian minority in Israel.

His novels are a living reminder of the struggle posed by the colonial nature of Israel in Palestinian society. As a Palestinian Arab, Habibi wrestled with reconciling his loyalty to the Palestinian people and its internationally recognized rights with his (then Communist Party–inspired) de facto recognition of the state of Israel, following the lead of the Soviet Union.

He began his literary work as a short story writer but in 1974 published what became his landmark opus, a short novel titled *The Strange Circumstances in the Disappearance of Sa'id the Luckless Pessoptimist.* An extraordinarily satirical novel that fuses fact with fantasy, it continues to be widely popular throughout the Arab World because of its wit, use of literary illusions, and originality. It is written in stream-of-conscious style and differs from other Arab novels in its heavy use of satire and sarcasm.

Following the life of Sa'id, the pessoptimist (a neologism he created that describes one who is simultaneously a pessimist and an optimist), the hero of the story from Galilee, Habibi brilliantly presents an interpretation of the catastrophe that led to the destruction of Palestine and the rise of Israel in its place. For the Palestinians who managed to stay behind and become second-class citizens of the state of Israel in which overnight they became an oppressed minority in their homeland, the hero of the *Pessoptimist* finds a world with norms that "defy the laws of nature and the imperatives of reason."[35] For many, this stunning novel is the most brilliant literary product of the modern Palestinians—not only for its brilliant and astonishing satire but also for its remarkable linguistic innovations, especially the neologisms in the title and the text but also because of the "juxtaposition of synonyms and antonyms with ironic undertones based on slight contextual differences in meaning (that) enhances the humor and satirical thrust."[36]

In his later life, Habibi was sharply criticized by both Palestinians and Israelis. On the Palestinian side, he was admonished for his surprising acceptance, in person, of an Israeli prize for literature from the Israeli prime minister. Israelis likewise criticized him for accepting a similar prize from Yasser 'Arafat, leader of the PLO. His biography was filmed just before his death from colon cancer in the 1996.

Liana Badr (1950–)

Another prominent female writer, Liana Badr is well known for the lyrical nature of her writing. Born into a nationalist family in Jerusalem in 1950, Liana Badr spent her childhood in Jericho until the invading Israeli tanks forced her family into exile in 1967. Her family resettled as refugees in Jordan, which she later left to obtain a bachelor's degree from Beirut Arab University in psychology and philosophy. Unfortunately, because of the Lebanese civil war, she was unable to continue in her goal to earn a master's degree. Like Sahar Khalifeh, she is a feminist who has worked with many organizations designed to assist Palestinian women in dealing both with Israeli occupation and the norms of a traditional society. In 1982, Badr took part in the mass migration of Palestinian refugees from Lebanon, traveling and living all over the Arab World until she returned to the West Bank in 1994, after the Oslo Accord was signed. Currently she resides in Ramallah with her husband and two daughters, where she runs the Cinema Department at the Palestinian Ministry of Culture.

Her major works include *A Compass for the Sunflower* (1979), which follows the life of a Palestinian woman forced into refugee status in both Amman and Beirut; *Balcony Over the Fakahani* (1983), composed of three novellas that each tell a different story of exile and resistance woven throughout the three major military losses in Palestine; *The Eye of the Mirror* (1991), an epic novel that tells the story of a Palestinian woman both before and after the massacre at the Tel Zaatar refugee Camp in Lebanon; and *Stars of Jericho* (1993), which has received wide international acclaim. She has also published several volumes of short stories, a volume of poetry, five children's books, and a biography of the poet Fawda Touqan. Badr is best known for her beautiful writing style, and many of her books have been translated into English.

Other authors that are internationally recognized include Samira Azzam, Yahya Yakhlef, Tawfiq Fayyad, and Antone Shammas, who writes in Hebrew, not Arabic.

ESSAYISTS AND INTELLECTUALS

Palestinians since al-Nakba have distinguished themselves as scholars, essayists, and nonfiction writers. Many have become journalists, columnists, essayists, and scholars in academic settings. Their writings have been printed not only in Palestinian publications but also in major Arabic- and English-language publications. Indeed, articulate Palestinian intellectuals, journalists, essayists, and scholars, writing in varied media and in different contexts, have come to be seen as the political conscience of the Arab World. Their efforts have contributed significantly to keeping alive the question of Palestine and the rights of its people both in the Arab world and in international public opinion

The contributions of three renowned writers—Edward W. Said, Naseer Aruri, and Hisham Sharabi—are appraised here. They have distinguished themselves not merely because of their insight into the Palestinian question but also because their contributions have universal relevance.

Edward W. Said (1934–2003)

The most famous of the essayists and intellectuals is Edward W. Said, who was University Professor of English and Comparative Literature at Columbia University in New York. For his distinguished career, Columbia University established a Chair in his name, the first named chair established while the person was still alive. Said, who died September 25, 2003, had an exceptionally distinguished academic and intellectual career. He wrote more than 20 books, and many have been translated into numerous languages, including nearly all the Western European languages, Japanese, Arabic, Farsi, and Urdu. His most influential work is *Orientalism*,[37] published in 1978, which single-handedly transformed the assumptions, framework, and structure of Western Middle Eastern Studies. It forced a paradigm shift not only in Middle Eastern studies but also Third World studies in general. This book and Said's later works launched a new field of intellectual and academic endeavor: postcolonial studies.

Orientalism is a study of how and why the West, and especially the United States, views the (Arab and Muslim) Orient. Said argued that these views developed in Europe and the United States over a long period of time and evolved as self-serving perceptions that had little to do with the more complex and rich reality of the Arab and Muslim Orient. It is as if the West created Orientalist views by itself and for itself with little regard to the reality of the Orient. The Orient, according to Said, is seen in the West as the opposite or negative "other" to the virtuous Western "self." Thus, the Western good self is practically defined in opposition to the evil Oriental other. Indeed, the positive self-image of the West is only possible as the mirror image of the negative Orient other. This self–other dichotomy is central to understanding Western views of the East. Such views and assumptions are rarely tested and are typically treated as self-evident perceptions that need no confirmation.

Over the centuries, argued Said, negative cultural, social, and political views of the Orient emerged and became consolidated into a dominant discourse that permeates all cultural domains, social institutions, and power centers in Western societies. It is this discourse, perceived as self-evident, that allows negative depictions and characterizations of Arabs, Muslims, and other Orientals (non-Westerners) to go unchallenged in the media, ranging from comic books (see *The Comic Book Arab*[38]) to movies (see *Reel Bad Arabs*[39]) to news coverage (*Covering Islam: How the Media and Experts Determine How We See the Rest of the World*),[40] to academic tomes,[41] doctoral dissertations, and even politician's political statements. The discourse is so embedded in the culture that it creates a veritable stereotype, often racist in content, that seems unshakable and unchallengeable. Although long in the making, the Western negative and hostile discourse on Arabs and Islam has received significant reinforcement in the recent past, most importantly because of the uneven Western portrayal of the Arab-Israeli conflict and specifically the Palestinian-Israeli struggle. Of course more recently, this discourse received quantum intensification as a result of the September 11, 2001, terrorist attacks on the World Trade Towers in New York and the Pentagon in Washington, DC. Horrific and condemnable as these attacks, perpetrated by 19 Arabs, were, the Orientalist discourse has allowed the characterization of *all* Arabs (280 million of them) and *all* Muslims (1.2 billion of them) as terrorists and evil. The dilemma of the Orientalist discourse is that it is not a mere prejudicial and stereotypical view of Palestinians, Arabs, and Muslims held by a minority in the West; it is the fact that this discourse permeates Western political culture and has probably influenced foreign policy deliberations toward the region.[42]

In addition to *Orientalism*, the works of Edward Said are many and include brilliant studies in literary criticism, such as *Culture and Imperialism* and *Power, Politics and Culture*, and considerations of the social and political role of the intellectual, such as *The World, the Text and the Critic* and *Representation of the Intellectual: The 1993 Reith Lectures*. Edward Said also wrote an acclaimed autobiography, *Out of Place*, while he was in the hospital for treatment of the cancer to which he eventually succumbed.

Naseer Aruri (1934–)

A major Palestinian intellectual, Naseer Aruri is Chancellor Professor Emeritus of political science at the University of Massachusetts, Dartmouth. He has authored numerous books and academic and opinion articles. He has written on a number of issues including human rights, especially in Israel; the occupied Palestinian territories; and the Arab World. Aruri was a member of the Board of

Amnesty International USA and Human Rights Watch/Middle East and an exemplary scholar-activist. Aruri founded, helped to found, or presided over a number of academic, research, and human rights organizations, including the Association of Arab-American University Graduates (AAUG), the Trans-Arab Research Institute (TARI), and the Arab Human Rights Organization that is based in Cairo and Geneva.

One of his early works is *Israel over Palestine*, a study of Israeli occupation of the Palestinian territories. It is a study of Israel's occupation policies, including the colonial settlements in the West Bank and Gaza Strip. This study was an early warning of the crucial issue, Israeli settlements in the Occupied Territories, that has become a major obstacle to peace in the Holy Land.

Aruri is an acclaimed scholar and analyst of American foreign policy toward the Middle East and of the Palestine question in particular. He has distinguished himself through numerous publications, especially two books on this question: *Obstruction of Peace* and *Dishonest Broker: The U.S. Role in Israel and Palestine*.[43] In these books, Aruri analyzes in detail the policy and actions of the U.S. Government in the "Peace Process" and how it is at odds with its declared position. He further demonstrates how U.S. policy has emerged as part of the problem rather than the solution to the Palestinian-Israeli conflict. Recently, Aruri edited *Palestinian Refugees: The Right of Return*. This timely book details the historical, legal, and international humanitarian rights of the Palestinian refugees, the apparently forgotten majority of the Palestinian people, many of whom are living in exile with few, if any, rights, including the right to compensation for properties lost in 1948. Aruri is also writing an autobiography. Like Edward Said, he is widely viewed as the conscience of the Palestinian cause both in America and in the Arab World.

Hisham Sharabi (1926–)

The Umar Al-Mukhtar Professor Emeritus of History at Georgetown University, Hisham Sharabi is the author of many books on Arab history, politics, and culture, including *Arab Intellectuals and the West: The Formative Years, 1975–1914* and *Theory, Politics and the Arab World*, an edited book that critically addresses scholarly views and assumptions of the various Western academic disciplines that address the Arab world. He has also written a multivolume autobiography in Arabic that has received critical acclaim in the Arab world. He founded and chaired the Jerusalem Fund, a philanthropic organization that provides assistance to Palestinians under Israeli occupation and the Palestine Center, a Washington think tank on Palestinian issues.

His signature work is *Neopatriarchy*.[44] It is a study of sociopolitical culture of the Arab World. Sharabi argues that the Arab World is caught in a culture that is neither traditional and patriarchal in character, nor modern, rational, and scientific in ethos. Rather, he argues that the contemporary culture of the Arab World, including that of the Palestinians, is neopatriarchal. Neopatriarchy is a hybrid culture caught between and combining aspects of traditionalism and modernity. It is sustained and reproduced in the Arab World as a result of the presence of self-serving traditional Arab elites and Western imperial intervention in the region. Neopatriarchy, according to Hisham Sharabi, operates as the ethos governing the structure of relationships and the behavior of Arabs in all the institutions of Arab societies—from the small family unit to the system of government. Sharabi believes that the Arab World and the rest of the Middle East will only be able to develop and achieve its unique version of modernity if it overcomes its neopatriarchal culture.

NOTES

1. Issa J. Boullata, "Literature," in *Encyclopedia of the Palestinians*, ed. Philip Mattar (New York: Facts on File, 2000), pp. 263–68.

2. David Barsamian, "An Interview with Edward W. Said," *Z Magazine*, February 1992, p. 90.

3. Hanan Mikhail-Ashrawi, "The Contemporary Literature of Palestine, Poetry and Fiction" (Ph.D. diss., Department of English, University of Virginia, 1982), p. 3.

4. Inea Bushnaq, "Folklore," in Mattar, *Encyclopedia of the Palestinians*, p. 133.

5. Ibid.

6. Mikhail-Ashrawi, "Contemporary Literature of Palestine," p. 19.

7. Ibid., p. 6.

8. Ben Bennani, *Psalms, Poems by Mahmud Darwish* (Colorado Springs, CO: Three Continents Press, 1994), p. 13.

9. From Jabra Ibrahim Jabra, "The Rebels, the Committed, and the Others: Transitions in Modern Arabic Poetry Today," *Middle East Forum* 43, no. 1 (1967): p. 20, cited in Bennani, *Psalms, Poems*.

10. Lawrence Joffe, "Fadwa Tuqan, Palestinian Poet Who Captured Her Nation's Sense of Loss and Defiance," *The Guardian*, 15 December 2003, www.guardian.co.uk/israel/Story/0,2763,1107273,00.html.

11. Maya Jaggi, "Mahmoud Darwish, Poet of the Arab World," *The Guardian*, 8 June 2002.

12. Ibid.

13. Carolyn Forche, in Mahmoud Darwish, *The Adam of Two Lost Edens, Poems* (Syracuse, NY: Syracuse University Press and Jusoor, 2000), back cover.

14. Jaggi, "Mahmoud Darwish," p. 2.

15. Ibid.

16. Munir Akash, "Introduction," in Darwish, *The Adam of Two Lost Edens*, p. 28.

17. Ibid., pp. 27, 33.

18. Bennani, *Psalms, Poems*, p. 18.

19. Akash, "Introduction," p. 39.

20. Jaggi, "Mahmoud Darwish."

21. Akash, "Introduction," p. 25.

22. Ashrawi, *Contemporary Literature of Palestine*, pp. 15, 20.

23. Ibid., pp. 64–65.

24. Ibid., p. 204.

25. Ibid., pp. 206–7.

26. Ibid., pp. 209, 213.

27. Ibid., p. 233.

28. Barbara Harlow, "Palestine or Andalusia: The Literary Response to the Israeli Invasion of Lebanon," *Race and Class* 2, no. 26 (1984): 41.

29. Sahar Khalifeh, *Women of No Man's Land,* original novel with introduction and critique (Ph.D. thesis, University of Iowa, 1988), p. 37.

30. Khalifeh, *Women,* p. 42.

31. Samaa Abu Sharar and Ghassan Joha, interview, 26 November 1998, http://archives.star.arabia.com/981126/JO5.html.

32. Ibid., p. 5.

33. Eisa Abu Shamsieh, "Jabra Ibrahim Jabra's Fiction" (Ph.D. diss., Indiana University, 1987), p. 242.

34. *The Ship* can be found in a translation by Adnan Haydar and Roger Allen (Boulder CO: Lynne Rienner, 1995), who also translated *In Search of Walid Masoud* (Syracuse, NY: Syracuse University Press, 2000).

35. Ashrawi, *Contemporary Literature of Palestine,* p. 276.

36. Ibid., p. 278.

37. E. W. Said, *Orientalism* (New York: Pantheon Books, 1978).

38. Jack Shaheen, "The Comic Book Arab," *The Link* 24, no. 5 (November–December, 1991).

39. Jack Shaheen, *Reel Bad Arabs* (Gloucestershire, UK: Arris, 2003).

40. Edward W. Said, *Covering Islam: How the Media and Experts Determine How We See the Rest of the World* (New York: Vintage, 1997).

41. Hisham Sharabi, ed., *Theory, Politics and the Arab World: Critical Responses* (New York: Routledge, 1990).

42. Edward W. Said, *The End of the Peace Process: Oslo and After* (New York: Vintage, 2001).

43. Naseer H. Aruri, *Dishonest Broker: The U.S. Role in Israel and Palestine* (Cambridge, MA: South End Press, 2003).

44. Hisham Sharabi, *Neopatriarchy* (New York: Oxford University Press, 1992).

7
Art, Performing Arts, and Cinema

The principal practices of Palestinian visual art are old and derive from the Islamic tradition. As Islam emerged as a faith condemning idolatry, it placed a prohibition against the creation of statues (idols), pictorial representation of humans, the Prophet Muhammad and his companions, and, above all, Allah. Accordingly, Islamic art evolved with a unique emphasis on abstract geometric and floral designs and on calligraphy in diverse venues. Calligraphy was used in architectural decorative motifs on the walls and ceilings of mosques and public buildings and in craftwork, especially copper and brass artifacts, glazed pottery, and illuminated books including the Qur'an. This architectural tradition is expressed in the stunning decorations both inside and on the outside the Dome of the Rock Mosque in Jerusalem. Although it is known for its shining golden dome, the mosque also exhibits some of the finest abstract geometric designs and beautiful calligraphy of passages from the Qur'an. Many other mosques in Palestine also exhibit similar artistic decorations.

The Dome of the Rock Mosque was built in the seventh century and has been renovated several times since then. Each time the decorations were enhanced and developed further. One of the leading Palestinian Islamic-style artists was Jamal Badran (1909–1999), who worked on the first major renovation of the mosque in the 1920s. Badran's reputation grew when he was commissioned to renovate the Minbar (pulpit) of the mosque after it was burned and destroyed by an extremist Israeli arsonist. He is also famous for individual pieces of Islamic art including illuminated glass, leather, lampshades, and other artifacts.

Palestinian history prior to the Islamic influence in the country was dominated by the Byzantine tradition with its pictorial iconography. Unlike the Western Catholic tradition, the eastern Christian churches eschewed statues depicting

Christ, the Virgin Mary, or the saints. Instead, eastern or Orthodox Christianity developed a tradition of pictorial iconography with two-dimensional patterns. This tradition may have not survived Islam and the Latin kingdoms of the medieval era because few churches were built after that time until the nineteenth century, when European missionaries built many new churches, including Roman Catholic, Greek Orthodox, and Russian Orthodox. As a result, visual art in the Byzantine tradition of icon paintings experienced a revival among Palestinian Christians. Small Icons found a ready market in Western pilgrims eager to buy portable mementos from the Holy Land for their homes and as gifts for their families and friends.[1] Larger icons, which decorated monastic and church sanctuaries, found a local and regional market throughout the nineteenth century as well.

Iconographers of the Jerusalem School, as it came to be known, may have learned the art from Greek and Russian monks who were resident in the holy land in the nineteenth century. However, its naturalization and distinguished Palestinian style had been evolving since the early eighteenth century. It is notable for

the almond shaped eyes and rounded facial features of the Arab folk hero of the period. The saddle of Saint George's horse, usually painted in a plain red, turns in the hands of a Jerusalem painter to crimson gilded in delicate stars and crescent . . . At times Greek may be the alphabet used to identify the icon's liturgical title; all other words, however, were usually painted in Arabic.[2]

PALESTINIAN FOLK ART

Palestinian folk art over the centuries was originally produced in items that were used in every day life such as pots, vases, drinking mugs, glasses, and pottery for storing water, grains and other such food products. Hebron (al-Khalil), for example, produced colorful pottery of all sizes and shapes with decorative designs typically floral in deep blue on a white glazed background. Gaza produced and sold widely beautiful glassware typically purple blue in color. Jerusalem families also produced glazed tile decorated with biblical or Qur'anic sayings. These traditions have survived into the present and have been commercially produced as souvenirs for the tourists. Since the eighteenth century, however, it is the olive-wood carvings and mother of pearl Christian religious items that have come to distinguish Palestinian folk art.

Olive-Wood Carvings

Woodcarvings and figurines are made from the branches of local olive trees. After the completion of the olive-picking season, the trees are pruned and the branches used for the famous carvings. Historians trace woodcarving as far back as the seventeenth century. Tradition has it that Franciscan monks, who arrived in Palestine during that century, helped train the native Christians in the art of carving. Accounts of European travelers to the Holy Land describe the beauty of

Glass blowing, Hebron. © E. Y. Farsakh

olive-wood rosaries, crucifixes, and other religious items and their popularity among Christian pilgrims. In addition to the olive-wood rosaries and crucifixes, Palestinian folk artists also produce the Nativity scene and individual figurines or statues of Mary, Joseph, and baby Christ in the manger, and the sheep, goats, cows, and donkeys that are traditionally included in the Nativity scene. Today carvers produce figures of camels, horses, and other local animals as well. The beauty of these handmade woodcarvings is enhanced by the multiple colors of the wood grain, which gives each figure a unique character. In the West Bank towns of Bethlehem, Beit Sahour, and Beit Jala, artisans continue to specialize in the production of olive-wood crosses, nativity sets, and statues of Christian saints.

Mother-of-Pearl

Mother-of-Pearl carving is another tradition that can be traced to the seventeenth century. Crosses, rosaries, and other wood carvings are often decorated with mother-of-pearl, and rosaries made from it evolved in response to the demands of Christian pilgrims, who came from Europe and Russia in increasing numbers in the nineteenth century. Mother-of-pearl is usually imported into Palestine from Saudi Arabia. In the contemporary period, the use of plastic for inlays in wood artifacts, especially in the manufacture of side tables, coffee tables, backgammon sets, and other artifacts has gained popularity. Both olive-wood and mother-of-pearl products still have a market among Western Christian pilgrims to the Holy Land.

MODERN ART

Modern painting began to develop in Palestine in the early twentieth century as Palestine increasingly came under European influence. A much stronger European influence arrived with the establishment of the Palestine British Mandate after World War I, which allowed practically unlimited immigration into the country of Jewish and Christian Europeans. Leading Palestinians talent of the time, like the icon painter Khalil Halaby, was largely self-taught in the European-inspired tradition. Artists primarily painted landscapes of their respective hometowns. Two women of the period received limited training: Nahil Bishara painted Palestinian figures in native dress, including embroidered garments, and Sophie Halaby painted typical Palestinian landscapes, often with stormy skies and the olive groves that define much of the central Palestinian countryside around Jerusalem, Bethlehem, and other towns.[3]

The developing Palestinian talent in modern art was cut short by the destruction and dismemberment of Palestine in 1948 and by the Israeli occupation of the West Bank and the Gaza Strip in 1967. Some artists were killed in the struggle against dispossession; others abandoned their interest or were unable to make a living from it. Two artists, however, continued to paint in exile: the multitalented novelist and short story writers Jabra Ibrahim Jabra in Baghdad and Ghassan Kanafani in Beirut.

Beginning in the mid-1950s, a second wave of exiled painters emerged in the refugee host countries and produced remarkable art. The earliest was Paul Guiragossian, an Armenian-Palestinian who combined biblical themes of exodus and exile to illuminate his personal ethnic and national worlds, the disinherited and dispossessed Palestinians, and the destitute and dispersed Armenians. Perhaps the most dramatic paintings and sketches of that era were those of Juliana Seraphim, born in Jaffa but living in exile in Beirut. Her work features unusual combinations of things (wild-flower petals, sculpted buds, seashells, and other products), winged beings, and fantastic creatures brought to life in imaginary orchards and other places.[4]

While these two artists followed their personal imaginations, Palestinian artists reared in refugee camps produced art that was far more socially and politically conscious. Like Palestinian poets, these painters used art to present and interpret their cause.[5] Like the literature of Palestine, its visual art focuses on the homeland and is often more political compared with the visual art of many traditions, especially those of Western countries. Diaspora Palestinian painters use art to tell the tragic story of Palestine and the Palestinians through easily understood symbols. The dream of returning to the homeland is thus expressed by paintings that depict its beauty. Ibrahim Ghannam's exquisite paintings clearly expressed this sentiment, and later, other artists, used the cactus plant that dots the Palestinian landscape and the key that symbolizes the lost homeland as symbols to indicate the undying wish to return home.

Another important theme in post-1948 Palestinian paintings was the painting of the cultural heritage. This tendency increased in importance as Palestinians began to observe the Israelis usurping Palestinian cultural heritage as their own.

For example, the national Israeli airline, El Al, started to dress its flight attendants with embroidered Palestinian dresses. Similarly, Israeli-owned restaurants overseas also started to sell typical Palestinian dishes, such as falafel, as their own national food. Palestinians that learned of such developments became outraged, and artists began to paint Palestinian objects and subjects as a way to assert their national identity and cultural heritage.[6] Indeed, the embroidered women's dress has been featured in the paintings of almost all artists. As the political movement for the liberation of the Palestinian homeland gathered momentum in the late 1960s, the brush, like the pen, became a weapon of political assertion. Representation of the guerrilla fighter and the gun in the period of intense political mobilization following al-Nakba and more so after the 1967 Arab-Israeli war became primary symbols of artistic and political resistance.[7]

Ismail Shamout

Ismail Shammout, who was expelled by Israeli forces from Lydda, southwest of Jerusalem, and journeyed on foot to a refugee camp in the Gaza Strip, won high recognition among Palestinians "for assimilating conventional verbal allegories into visual images." Reproductions of many of his paintings became common household decorations in the homes of people in refugee camps and inside businesses of Palestinians in the diaspora.[8] Some critics consider Shammout the founder of modern Palestinian art. He is prolific painter who has interpreted in both realistic and symbolic form the varied stages of the Palestinian struggle since the 1950s: the painful reality of al-Nakbah, the exodus, the massacres of innocent civilians, the possible resurrection in the rise of Palestinian resistance, the occupation, and Palestinian identity through portrayals of peasant women, and nostalgic idyllic depictions of Palestinian village life. For example, during the civil war in Lebanon, which involved Palestinian refugees living there, the Tel al-Zaatar refugee camp east of Beirut fell to right-wing Lebanese militias, and hundreds if not thousands of refugees were killed. In commemoration of that tragedy, Shamout painted *The Sun*, a defiant portrait of people with raised fists underneath a huge dramatic sun.

Naji al-Ali (1936–1987)

One of the most admired Palestinian artists—not only among the Palestinians but also other Arabs—was Naji al-Ali, who turned his drawings into the satirical art of political cartoons. Al-Ali's cartoons reflected Palestinian and Arab public opinion and were critical biting commentaries on Palestinian and Arab politics and political leaders. Each cartoon featured Hanzala (or Hanthala), a young spectator witnessing the activity in the cartoon satirizing a particular policy or event. In the art of Naji al-Ali, Hanzala was the intrepid witness to Arab and Palestinian history during al-Ali's lifetime. His stinging satire earned him the enmity of many political leaders. He was threatened in Beirut where he lived. As a result, he moved to London but was assassinated there by unknown assailants in 1987.

In 1988, he was awarded posthumously the International Federation of Newspaper Publishers' Golden Pen Award.

A third phase of Palestinian art developed in the wake of the Israeli conquest and occupation of the West Bank and the Gaza Strip, an event that accelerated Palestinians' aspirations to regain their homeland. Under the auspices of the new liberation movement spearheaded by the PLO, Palestinian artists in the diaspora founded a Union of Artists and helped organize group exhibits in many Arab countries. These included the innovative photo silkscreens by Layla Shawwa (1940–) and stylized engravings by Abd Al-Rahman Muzayyin (1943–).

Disconnected from the Arab surroundings until 1993, Palestinian artists in the Occupied Territories also established a separate League of Palestinian Artists. Individual and group exhibits under Israeli occupation quickly took on the political meaning of resistance to the occupation. Art exhibitions became community events that symbolized national identity and self-affirmation. Because of this all art exhibitions were banned and the Israeli authorities censored the simultaneous artistic use of the colors of the Palestinian flag—red, white, green, and black.[9]

Suleiman Mansour (1947–)

One leading artist in the Occupied Territories is Suleiman Mansour, whose style is full of metaphoric imagery. In one of his famous works, a rainbow pours through the bars of a prison window; once inside the prison cell, the rainbow turns into the four colors of the national Palestinian flag. Another of his works shows bent prison bars and a checkered dove with flaming wings dashing into the sun. Perhaps his most famous and most popularly reproduced painting is the *Camels of Hardship* (1973). It features an old man, a barefoot porter, carrying a stylized Jerusalem (symbolizing Palestine), with the Dome of the Rock in its center, on his back. For Palestinians, this painting symbolized the heavy burden of their cause and the fact that they carry their identity on their shoulders everywhere they live. With the start of the first Intifada in 1987, Mansour emerged as a new leader of the New Vision art movement, which boycotted Israeli products and started using local materials in artwork. Mud, clay, and natural dyes such as henna were used in paintings and mud sculptures of human figures. From the early 1990s—Mansour progressively abandoned color in his works and stopped using it altogether in 1996 when he lost all hope of the peace process producing an end to the Israeli occupation. Cracks have dominated his more recent work. To Mansour, the cracks "represent the destruction and ruin that the Palestinians suffer from."[10] This artistic innovation is best represented in a composition he titled *Shrinking Object*, which depicts one cracked map of historic Palestine inside another.

Samira Badran

More dramatic than Mansour's portrayals is the work of Samira Badran, who witnessed the Israeli conquest of the West Bank. This and the subsequent oppressive occupation have left an indelible impact on her psyche and artistic production. Badran's visual art is apocalyptic. In one highly dramatic painting, she presents flames in strong colors intermingling with miscellaneous bits of machinery next to dismembered body parts while humans who are whole are "caged, muzzled or strapped. In the distance, metal scaffolding of blown-up buildings reaches out to metallic skies."[11] This is a clear and powerful artistic rendition and condemnation of the consequences of occupation and control of Palestinians by Israel.

Kamal Boullata (1942–)

One of the most talented and innovative Palestinian artists is Kamal Boullata. Of his work, he says, "for years, [I] was fascinated by the square, geometric rendering of Arabic script. [I] composed fragments of text from Christian and Muslim sources in translucent colors and angular shapes, creating mandalas of Arabic in which reading becomes interchangeable with seeing."[12] In his later works, calligraphy disappeared, replaced with geometric compositions characterized by contrasting colors and fragmented angular forms that are refractory and seem to intensify ambiguities and enhance the imagination.[13] In short, Palestinian art has expressed imaginatively the catastrophic and continuing tragedy of Palestinian history and experiences. Boullata also wrote and illustrated a poignant book of children's art titled *Faithful Witness: Palestinian Children Recreate Their World*.[14]

Mona Hatoum (1952–)

Palestinian visual art has three principal sources of influence: first, its own ancient cultural traditions that date back to the art of the Canaanites and of pharaonic Egypt; second, medieval Arab Islamic geometric abstractions and the unique and elaborate calligraphy typically applied to architectural surfaces and copper and brass pots, drinking jugs, vases, utensils, and other artifacts; and, finally, modern art, especially cubist and installation art. The best and most famous representative of modern influences and contemporary innovative art among Palestinians is the artwork of Mona Hatoum. A renowned Palestinian artist living and working in London, Mona Hatoum has gained international recognition. She has generated enormous interest and excitement in the international art world. Astonishingly versatile, she works with a variety of materials (steel, glass, wire mesh, marble, rubber, human hair) and media (video, drawing, sculpture, installation art, performance art, and photography).

Born in 1952 in Beirut to a Palestinian refugee family, she studied art in Beirut but had to escape the Lebanese civil war, fleeing to London in 1975 where she continued her studies. Her early work was inspired by her exile from Beirut and that of her parents from Palestine. It also reflects her cultural displacement and her concern for gender and social injustice. Her work is both silently political and profoundly personal. One of Hatoum's works (*Present Tense*) is an excellent example of the personal and the political. The work is made of cubes of Nablus soap with red beads pressed into them. These represent West Bank Palestinian land that should have been turned over to the Palestinian Authority after the Oslo Accords.[15] Nablus, in the northern West Bank, has been famous for the production and export of olive-oil-based soap since the nineteenth century.

In 2000, Hatoum had an exhibit of her works titled "The Entire World as a Foreign Land," which investigated the relationship between individual identity and the sense of belonging to a broader cultural and geographic identity. In several of her constructions, borders of rooms are made of fencing, and furniture is indicated by contours in which most three-dimensional forms are transparent. Typically, Hatoum employs minimalist tools—formal symmetry, absence or significant reduction of color—with distortions of scale, magnification, and multiplication to produce dramatic intensity.[16] For example, one of her most famous works is *Corps etranger* (1994), a video of internal and external self-portrait of the artist features "an endoscopic journey through the artist's body"[17] accompanied by the magnified sounds of her stomach and heart. She draws the viewer into her art, "the familiar becomes grotesque and the grotesque reveals itself as familiar.[18]

Hatoum uses ordinary household objects, familiar shapes with pleasant spatial relationships that on closer inspection are actually far more complex. For example, her 1992–1993 installation titled *Socle du Monde* initially appears to be a solid black cube. On closer inspection, one sees "a network of iron filings attached to magnets and steel plates built into a cube-shaped frame."[19]

PERFORMING ARTS
Theater

The tradition of performing art goes back to Arab medieval times in Palestine and the region. In traditional village life, older members of the family and itinerant professional storytellers (*hakawatis*) embellished the stories with minimal use of costumes, gestures, and acting. A more formal theatre emerged in the nineteenth century and developed further in pre-Nakba Palestine. Whereas the urban middle class and Palestinian elite enjoyed Western-inspired theater productions in the major cities, villagers were entertained by itinerant actors who performed mime and improvisational performances inspired by everyday life of the village and by classical legends of Arab and Muslim battles and heroes, and romantic tragedies such as *Qais wa Lubna* and *Majnoun Laila*, the lover who became insane at the loss of his loved one. By the end of the British Mandate, Palestinian playwrights such as Jamal al-Bahri, Asma Toubi, Stephan Joseph Salim, and Nashi Al-Jawzi wrote and produced plays that were popular with Palestinian audiences. The latter wrote and produced several nationalist plays—among his most famous is *I Will Not Sell My Land*—that elicited the ire of the British colonial authorities. Al-Jawzi also created an association of theater artists and wrote *History of Palestinian Theater, 1918–1948*. Al-Nakba interrupted theatrical activity until the 1960s, however.

Under Israeli occupation Palestinian theatrical activity reemerged. One theater group was founded in 1969 in Ramallah. Al-Kasaba group was founded in 1970, al-Hakawati in 1973, and Sanabel in 1985. The Palestinian National Theater, an organization supported by the official Ministry of Culture of the Palestinian Authority, was also founded after the Oslo Accords were signed in 1993. Although the Palestinian theater groups produce many famous plays in translation from English and French, much of the local plays are nationalist in character reflecting the problems, dilemmas, and ironies of Palestinian life under occupation. At al-Hakawati Theater, for example, cabaret-style productions and plays are often political in content. Israeli occupation authorities frequently censor or unexpectedly shut down the production. Conscious of potential visiting Western audiences, English synopses are typically available at such performances. Many Westerners interested in the Palestinian society and culture visit this and other theaters and typically receive an artistic interpretation of Palestinian life under occupation.

In 1991, the first teaching theater in Palestine, the Ashtar for Theatre Productions and Training, was launched. It not only trains students in acting but also has a Drama Teachers Training Program. The first cohort of Drama Teachers graduated in 2003. Ashtar also launched the Drama Teachers Training program with private, government and UNRWA schoolteachers. It thus brought theater clubs for the first time into government and UNRWA schools. In 2000, Ashtar produced *Land and Sky*, the first professional play geared toward children. It also joined with al-Mir'at Media of Jordan and El-Teatro of Tunisia to produce *Of Soil and Crimson*, a play that was performed at Manger Square in Bethlehem as part of the second millennium celebrations.

In a project of the Al-Rowwad Theatre of the Aida Refugee Camp in the West Bank, six American playwrights visited Palestine and met with Palestinian playwrights and theater groups. The visit was organized by the American playwright Naomi Wallace, and Palestinian playwright Abdel-Fattah Abu-Srour, director of Al-Rowwad Theater. It took place after an initial visit by the Naomi Wallace and the British Director David Gothard who, accompanied by Abdel-Fattah Abu-Srour, made the first contacts with some of the Palestinian theater groups. The visiting playwrights included Tony Kushner, Lisa Schlesinger, Kia Corthron, Robert O'Hara, the Palestinian American Playwright Betty Shamieh, and Naomi Wallace. The American playwrights visited Ashtar Theatre in Ramallah, Deaf Theatre in Maghar, Inad Theatre in Beit Jala, Theatre Day Productions in Hebron and Gaza, and Al-Rowwad Cultural and Theatre Training Center for children in Aida Camp, near Bethlehem. They also met with playwright and director Adnan Tarabshi and playwright and director Reyad Massarwa.

Al-Kasaba Theater group, perhaps the most accomplished of those in the Occupied Territories, has been on tours in Europe and the United States. Its production of *Alive from Palestine: Stories under Occupation* comprising short scenes and monologues, was directed by Nizar Zubi and artistic director Abed Al-Jubeh. It received acclaim even from critics who are not familiar or sympathetic to the Palestinian dilemma of occupation.[20] The theater critic for the *New York Times* wrote that the stories they tell are those of legitimate experience; this is what it feels like to be an ordinary Palestinian now. And with that in mind, "Alive from Palestine" is valuable theater . . . the stories told by the actors . . . are full of the irony and pathos you would expect.[21]

Theater groups are many and have been active in many towns and villages and have become one of the few outlets of communities under siege of Israeli occupation troops in which children and community members and groups participate.

Songs and Music

Traditional Palestinian songs and music in the villages and rural areas of Palestine and the surrounding Arab countries are similar. Palestinians sing (and dance) on all the important, happy occasions such weddings, births, confirmation, and other rites of passage. They typically sing songs to tunes produced by traditional and classical Arab instruments. Each village has an informally recog-

Songs of Freedom Festival, Jerusalem. © Steve Sabella/Yobous Productions

nized singer or two who are frequently called on to sing. At weddings and religious holiday celebrations, Palestinian villagers often listened to musical renditions of spontaneous zajal poetry. The zajal singers and poetry readers, called *zajjaleen* (plural of *zajjal*), were, as noted earlier, itinerant professional singers and poets who go from village to village to perform. Although it is a dying custom under the Israeli occupation of the West Bank, it is still practiced in certain locations and on special occasions and in refugee camps among the diaspora Palestinians. Typically, peasants and farmers often sing while working in the fields.

Traditionally among the rural population of Palestine, several forms or types of songs are commonly and popularly known. These include 'Ataba, Dal'ona, Zajal songs, and Zaghareet, or women's songs. *Ataba* songs usually include four verses of poetry, the first three of which end with the same word sound but with different meanings. Typically, the fourth verse ends with a word ending in a sound like *aab*, *awa*, and so on.[22] They are usually sung by men. *Dal'ona* songs do not have the stylistic and poetic constraints of 'Ataba and are easier to compose and sing. Like 'Ataba, *Dal'ona* songs also typically comprise three verses that have somewhat similar endings while the fourth verse ends in a word or sound that has 'ona in it. *Zaghareet* are popular women's songs that are often intended to celebrate the occasion, for example, a wedding, a bride, the birth of a boy, or the family. The verses of the song are often short and end in an ululating sound by the lead singer and other women in the group.

Popular among all Palestinians, rural or urban, are classical Arab songs that hail from the medieval period, especially the Andalusian Arab era. These are beautiful melodic renditions in classical verse or poems. In the contemporary period, Palestinians listen to and sing modern songs of the eastern Arab world, especially the songs of Umm Kalthoum, Mohammad Abdul-Wahhab (both of Egypt), Fairouz and Wadie' Safi (of Lebanon), and many others who have been and are currently popular in the eastern Arab countries. Some of Fairuz's songs about Jerusalem (especially her song "Al-Qudsu Lana," Jerusalem Is Ours) and her Christian church hymns are particularly evocative of the Palestinian cause.

After 1948, many Palestinian musicians became refugees. These included Sabri Sharif (1922–1999) and the classical baritone Alvarez Boulos who established the Orpheus Choir in Lebanon. The composer Habib Hassan Touma (1934–) resided in Germany and became known for his Arabic ethnomusicology. Simon Shaheen took up residence in New York. Also important after 1967 is Adel Salameh. Under occupation in the West Bank, several singing groups and choral clubs appeared. One is the Sabreen choral group who perform internationally.

Dance

The traditional dance in the Arab countries of the eastern Mediterranean including Palestine is the *Dabke* (sometimes spelled *Debka*). The *Dabke* is a communal dance in which the dancers, usually segregated by gender, hold hands in a semicircle and dance to the rhythm of the music and occasionally stomp their feet in coordinated steps. The leader swirls a kerchief and leads the rest of the dancers in specific steps and rhythmic foot stomping. It is a joyous activity that is accompanied by whoops and other sounds of the dancers and the clapping of the audience or spectators. There are several dance variations in the *Dabke*. Various regions of Palestine have differing dance steps and songs and musical accompaniment to the *Dabke*. In the period after al-Nakba, the *Dabke* dance has taken on a cultural-political character because it is performed spontaneously by people at all kinds of celebration or political gatherings in the occupied Palestinian territories and among the diaspora communities. Palestinian immigrant gatherings in the United States also frequently feature the *Dabke*.

Other types of dance are more individual and performed to the appreciation and delight of the spectators of a given gathering. In the rural areas, one or two men in celebratory gatherings perform a ritual dance with a sword and (small) shield. Such dances are typically inspired by the great Arab and Islamic warriors of old. The sword is swung overhead and banged on the small round shield as the dancer steps rhythmically to music or even a poem being recited. A much more graceful dance is performed by the bride at her own wedding ceremony to the rhythm called "one and a half" beat. After the bride dances, others join in spontaneously, competing with each other for attention and applause.

Beginning in the 1960s, dance among the Palestinian communities under occupation and in the diaspora has evolved in a more structured manner. Dance troupes were founded and trained young dancers in choreography inspired by the traditional Palestinian styles and influenced by Western, especially American, dance theater. One of the most important Palestinian troupes is *El-Funoun* (the Arts). Founded in 1979 by dancers, it aspired to produce traditional Palestinian dance in a modern style and perspective. It has contributed to efforts against the marginalization of children and youth in the context of a highly politicized struggle against Israeli occupation. This, along with youth-oriented theater, gives the children of Palestine the opportunity to express their cultural identity and explore their traditions in an artistic and inspiring way.

Another dance troupe that has gained reputation is *Bara'em*. Established in 1984, its principal objectives include promoting the talents and creativity of Palestinian children and youths and providing for them positive role models. In addition, it hopes to present to the international community a positive image of Palestinian youth. The majority of the members of the troupe are students who have studied Dabke at the Popular Arts Center in the city of Ramallah. Like El-Funoun, the Bara'em troupe also produces dance performances that are based in the traditional dance of Palestine but inspired by the development of modern choreography.

CINEMATOGRAPHY

Cinematography is a recent artistic development among the Palestinians. The earliest beginnings were the production of documentary films produced by directors affiliated with the PLO. One of the earliest is Mustafa Abu-Ali (1938–2001) who founded the film division or unit (Wahdat Aflam Filasteen) in 1968 when the PLO was based in Jordan. In September 1970, an estimated 20,000 Palestinians were killed in the civil war between the Palestinian guerillas and the Jordanian army in Amman, Jordan. In the wake of Black September, Abu-Ali moved along with the PLO to Lebanon. There he continued producing such documentaries as *They Have No Existence* (1974), *Tel al-Za'tar* (1975), *Palestine in the Eye* (Filastin fi'l 'Ayn) (1977), and others. In addition to Abu-Ali, the distinguished painter Ismail Shamout also produced documentary films as part of the cultural and political activity of the PLO. Among the early others were Qasim Hawl and Rafi Hajjar. Qasim Hawl branched out in the 1980s into making feature films. His best known is the feature film *Return to Haifa* ('Aa'id ila Hayfa) (1982).

Since then, a veritable explosion in Palestinian filmmaking has developed. Many of these filmmakers live in the United States, Western Europe, or in the occupied territories. They have been making documentaries, feature films, and other products. The following paragraphs review the works of some of the most prominent young filmmakers, some of whom are also actors.

Mai Masri (1948–)

Originally from the West Bank city of Nablus, Masri is based principally in Beirut and London. She received a degree in film production from San Francisco State University and has directed and produced several award-winning films that have been shown internationally. Her filmography includes *Frontiers of Dreams and Fears* (2001), a poignant documentary that follows the tenuous friendship that develops between two young Palestinian girls, one a resident of the destitute refugee camps in the greater Beirut area and the other a resident of a large refugee camp near Bethlehem in the Occupied Territories, who establish a relationship through correspondence. They eventually meet face to face across a fence at the Lebanese border after the Israeli occupation forces withdraw. Soon, however, their lives are disrupted as the Palestinian Intifada against Israeli occupation of the West Bank and Gaza Strip occurs.[23] Another of Masri's excellent documentaries is *Hanan Ashrawi: A Woman of Her Time* (1995), which is an account of the life with interviews of the internationally celebrated Palestinian professor, writer, spokesperson, and human rights activist.

Children of Shatila (1998) is a documentary on the children of the Shatila Refugee Camp on the outskirts of Beirut, which suffered horrendous genocidal killings at the hands of a right-wing Lebanese militia under the control of the Israeli army during the Israeli siege of the city of Beirut in the summer of 1982. The documentary features Farah, an 11-year-old girl, and Issa, a 12-year-old boy, and how the children of the camp, a third generation since 1948 when the camp was founded, come to terms with their difficult and tragic reality of living in a camp that has suffered a vicious massacre, a debilitating siege, unemployment and starvation. The director gave the children video cameras and allowed them to tell the story of the camp in their own words.[24]

Michel Khleifi (1950–)

Born in Nazareth in 1950, Khleifi studied television and theater directing in Belgium. His feature films include *Fertile Memory* (1980), *Canticle of the Stones* (1990), *L'Ordre du Jour* (1993), and *Tale of the Three Jewels* (1995). *Tale* is an allegory of a Palestinian boy, Youssef, who becomes smitten with a gypsy girl, Aida, who will return his love only if he is able to find the lost jewels of her grandmother. Set against the backdrop of the Palestinian Intifada in Gaza, Youssef "embarks on a mystical pursuit, which leads him to a wise old man, a mysterious scroll, death, and resurrection."[25] Khlefi's most celebrated film, however, is *Wedding in Galilee* (1987), which won the International Critics Prize at the Cannes Film Festival. *Wedding in Galilee* is a classic in Palestinian feature filmmaking. It tells the story of a traditional Palestinian wedding that is affected in interesting ways by the intrusion of a local Israeli military commander who grants the permit for holding the wedding celebration only with the condition that he be invited. His presence forces the celebration to concentrate on him.

Elia Suleiman (1960–)

Also born in Nazareth, Elia Suleiman has lived in New York, the Netherlands, and France, as well as in Palestine. His filmography includes *Cyber-Palestine* (1999), a feature film that tells the story of a modern-day Joseph and Mary who live in Gaza and try to reach Bethlehem at the turn of the new millennium, but to arrive on time would be a miracle. It is a commentary on the tragedy of Palestinian life under occupation. Elia Suleiman's film, *Chronicle of a Disappearance* (1996), received Best First Feature Award in the 1996 Venice Film Festival. The film addresses the question of what it means to be Palestinian since al-Nakba of 1948. To answer the question, Suleiman, who had been living in New York City, returns to his homeland to rediscover his roots in the Palestinian Arab culture that has been effectively uprooted by Israel. *Chronicle of a Disappearance* is a reflection "on the spiritual effect of political instability on the Palestinian psyche."[26] Other films include *War and Peace in Vesoul* (1997), and an experimental video film titled *Introduction to the End of an Argument* (Bidayat al-Nihayat al-Jidal), co-directed with Jayce Salloume (1990). Suleiman and Salloume use clips from Hollywood feature films, cartoons, and TV to critique the portrayal of Arabs in American and European media and its effects on foreign policy. These clips are juxtaposed with scenes shot in the West Bank along with text.[27]

Suleiman's latest film is *Divine Intervention* (2002). Set in the West Bank, the film tells a love story of a Palestinian man living in Jerusalem and a Palestinian woman living in the nearby town of Ramallah. The man struggles with his obligation to care for his ailing father and returning to the relationship with the woman. More problematic for the romantic relationship is that she is barred from crossing the checkpoint into Jerusalem. They resort to making loving in a vacant lot next to the Israeli checkpoint. With the siege of Palestine cities intruding on their lives, "a complicity of solemn desire begins to generate violent repercussions and, against the odds, their angry hearts counter-attack with spasms of spectacular fantasy."[28] The film won the Jury Prize at the 2002 Cannes Film Festival.

Other Filmmakers

The Web site of an American organization called Dream of a Nation, which is attempting to archive and create a network of connections to access and feature Palestinian films, lists more than 60 Palestinian filmmakers producing documentary, feature, and video films on practically all continents, including North America and Latin America. These are gifted, well-trained, and creative filmmakers, some of whom are also actors. Their productions are innovative, documenting real-life Palestinian experiences in varied eras and formats. For example, Kais al-Zobaidi's documentary *Palestine, a People's Record* is an extraordinary video of the history of Palestine from 1917 to 1974 that includes compelling archival footage gathered from numerous sources. It stands as an excellent testament to the modern history of the country up to that year.[29]

Najwa Najjar produced *Na'im wa Wadee'a* (1999), a documentary that explores social life in the city of Jaffa before 1948 through a portrait of a Palestinian couple, Wadee'a Aghabi and Na'im Azar. It is constructed through oral histories presented by their daughters and relatives. It won a prize at the 2000 Hamptons International Film Festival.[30] Similarly, *Blanche's Homeland* (2001), a film by Maryse Gargour that traces the succession of exiles of an elderly woman who, along with her parents was first exiled from Jaffa to become a refugee in the wake of the 1948 Nakba. Blanche is shown disappointed and dismayed at a world that has turned its back on Palestine and Palestinian rights. But, "through dialogues between younger generations of exiled Palestinians, [Blanche] bears witness to the tenacity and permanence of their identity.[31] These are intimate, evocative films made by a new generation of Palestinians about the lives and experiences of those who lived through al-Nakba and continue to suffer from its consequences.

Other young filmmakers are producing feature films. One of the more innovative is *The Moon Sinking* by Ahmad Habash (2001). This film depicts the story of the last days of seven ordinary people just before the moon is about to collide with earth, destroying all things.[32]

In his first feature film, *The Olive Harvest*, writer and director Hanna Elias tells a complex Palestinian love story about two brothers who compete for the love of a woman. One brother wants to stay on the land and harvest olives; the other, just out of an Israeli prison, wants to become a member of the Palestinian Legislative Council. The movie "explores the dynamics of human relationships between brother and brother, woman and man, father and daughter, sister and sister, and person to land."[33]

Palestinian-American Annemarie Jacir produced an innovative fictional film, *The Satellite Shooters* (2001) in the style of an American Western. A Palestinian boy in Texas teams up with a local gunslinger, the Kid, to change the world. The Satellite Shooters was the Official Selection of the 2002 Tous Courts International Film Festival.[34]

In conclusion, despite the varying trajectories of the social and political history of the three major segments of the Palestinian population since 1948 and the arrival of three new generations since then, the cultural production in all areas—music, song, dance, theater, and film—continues to focus on similar themes, especially the oppressive occupation and the denial of rights and identity. The Palestinian question continues to be central to the international diplomatic agenda precisely because of the unyielding commitment and activism of the Palestinian people. Lasting peace in the Middle East will be difficult to achieve without justice for the Palestinians.

NOTES

1. This section is based on an article by Kamal Boullata, "Art," in *Encyclopedia of the Palestinians*, ed. Philip Mattar (New York: Facts on File, 2000), pp. 67–73.

2. Ibid., p. 67.

3. Ibid., p. 68.

4. Ibid.

5. Ibid.

6. Samia A. Halaby, "Contemporary Palestinian Art," http://village.infoweb.ne.jp/~fwjh7903/palestinian_contemporary_art.htm.

7. Ibid.

8. Boullata, "Art," p. 70.

9. Ibid., p. 71.

10. Khalil Sakakini Cultural Centre, "Suliman Mansoour," http://www.Sakakini.org.

11. Boullata, "Art," p. 71.

12. Ibid., p. 72.

13. Ibid.

14. Kamal Boullata, *Faithful Witness: Palestinian Children Recreate Their World* (New York: Olive Branch Press, 1990).

15. Anne Martens, "Mona Hatoum," Museum of Contemporary Art (MOCA), 22 June–3 August 2003, http://artscenecal.com/ArticlesFile/Archive/Articles2003/Articles 0703/MHatoumA.html.

16. Laura Cottingham, "Mona Hatoum," http://www.artpace.org/whatsnew/PR.jhtml?ID=47&Previous=press.jhtml.

17. "Mona Hatoum," Tate Gallery, London, 24 March–23 July 2000, http://www.absolutearts.com/artnews/2000/03/26/26746.html.

18. "Mona Hatoum," Art and Culture Network, http://www.abu-ali.com/aae/hatoshow.htm.

19. Ibid.

20. Robert Hurwitt, "Palestinians Tell Their Side in 'Alive', Ramallah Troupe Moving, Provocative," *San Francisco Chronicle*, 9 July 2002.

21. Bruce Weber, "A Plea for Recognizing Humanity Everywhere," *New York Times*, 27 June 2002, http://www.nytimes.com/2002/06/27/arts/theater/27ALIV.html.

22. "Palestinian Popular Songs," www.barghouti.com/folklore/songs.

23. See the Dreams of a Nation Web site: http://dreamsofanation.org/films.html.

24. Ibid.

25. Ibid.

26. Ibid.

27. Ibid.

28. Ibid.

29. Ibid.

30. Ibid.

31. Ibid.

32. Ibid.

33. Ibid.

34. Ibid.

Appendix

Table A.1
Settlements in the Gaza Strip

Name	Population 2001***	Population 2000**	Population 1999*	Date of Establishment
Bedolah		184	197	1982/1986+
Bene Azmon		497	475	1979
Dugit		61	53	1990*
Ele Sinai		334	324	1982
Gadid		289	259	1982
Gan Or		267	261	1982/1983+
Gannei Tal		287	277	1979/1977+
Katif		317	296	1978
Kfar Darom		244	242	1970/1990+
Kfar Yam		N/A	N/A	N/A
Morag		146	142	1982/1987/1972+
Netzarim		347	297	1980/1992/1972+
Neve Dekalim	2,400	2,280	2,230	1982/1983/1980+
Netzar Hazzani		312	301	1973/1977+
Nisanit		874	750	1985/1984/1982+
Pe'at Sadeh		110	106	1989*
Rafiah Yam		129	127	1984
Total	2,400	6,678	6,337	

Note: These data are constantly revised by the Foundation for Middle East Peace, www.fmep.org.

+ The first date is given by the Settlement Division of the Zionist Organization. The second date is given by the Yesha Council of Jewish Communities in Judea, Samaria, and Gaza. The third date is from Peace Now.

* Source: List of Localities: Their Population and Codes, 31.12.1999. Jerusalem: Central Bureau of Statistics, 2000.

** Source: List of Localities: Their Population and Codes, 31.12.2000. Jerusalem: Central Bureau of Statistics, 2001.

*** Source: List of Localities: Their Population and Codes, 31.12.2001. Jerusalem: Central Bureau of Statistics, 2002.

Table A.2
Settlements in the Gaza Strip by Population ~1999–2001

Name	Population 2001***	Population 2000**	Population 1999*	Date of Establishment
Neve Dekalim	2,400	2,280	2,230	1982/1983/1980+
Nisanit		874	750	1985/1984/1982+
Bene Azmon		497	475	1979
Netzarim		347	297	1980/1992/1972+
Ele Sinai		334	324	1982
Katif		317	296	1978
Netzar Hazzani		312	301	1973/1977+
Gadid		289	259	1982
Gannei Tal		287	277	1979/1977+
Gan Or		267	261	1982/1983+
Kfar Darom		244	242	1970/1990+
Bedolah		184	197	1982/1986+
Morag		146	142	1982/1987/1972+
Rafiah Yam		129	127	1984
Pe'at Sadeh		110	196	1989*
Dugit		61	53	1990*
Kfar Yam		N/A	N/A	N/A
Total	2,400	6,678	6,337	

Note: These data are constantly revised by the Foundation for Middle East Peace, www.fmep.org.

* Source: List of Localities: Their Population and Codes, 31.12.1999. Jerusalem: Central Bureau of Statistics, 2000.

** Source: List of Localities: Their Population and Codes, 31.12.2000. Jerusalem: Central Bureau of Statistics, 2001.

*** Source: List of Localities: Their Population and Codes, 31.12.2001. Jerusalem: Central Bureau of Statistics, 2002.

Table A.3
Settlements in East Jerusalem

Name	Population 2000	Area (dunums)
Giv'at Ha-Mivtar	2,912	588
Ma'alot Dafna, Kiryat Arye	3,645	380
Ramat Eshkol	2,917	397
Sanhedriyya Ha-Murhevet	5,018	378
Ramat Shlomo	11,348	1,126
Har Ha-Hozvim (industrial zone)	0	653
Ramot Allon	37,934	4,979
Neve Ya'akov	20,288	1,759
Pisgat Ze'ev	36,469	5,467
Giv'at Shapira	8,193	2,018
East Talpiot	12,845	1,195
Gilo	27,637	2,859
Giv'at Ha-Matos and Har Homa	763	310/2,523
Old City-Jewish Quarter	2,279	122
Total	172,248	24,754

Source: Statistical Yearbook of Jerusalem No. 19, 2001.

Table A.4
Settlements in the West Bank [Regional names are those given to the West Bank areas by Israel.

Name	Population 2001***	Population 2000**	Population 1999*	Date of Establishment	Region
Adora		271	291	1983	Mount Hebron
Alei Zahav		391	355	1982	Samaria
Alfei Menashe	5,000	4,580	4,410	1983	Samaria
Allon Shevut	2,900	2,680	2,230	1970	Etzion Bloc
Almog		167	156	1977	Jordan Valley
Almon		698	672	1982	Benjamin
Argaman		164	155	1968	Jordan Valley
Ariel	16,000	15,600	15,100	1978	Samaria
Asfar (Metzad)		361	356	1984	Mount Hebron
Ateret		302	287	1981	Benjamin
Avnei Hefetz		785	695	N/A	Samaria
Barkan		1,150	1,080	1981	Samaria
Beit Arye		2,380	2,330	1981	Samaria
Beit El		4,120	3,800	1977	Benjamin
Beit ha'Arava		55	45	1980	Jordan Valley
Beit Horon		772	720	1977	Benjamin
Benjamin					
Beqa'ot		144	144	1972	Jordan Valley
Betar 'Illit	17,300	15,800	12,700	1985	Etzion Bloc
Bitronot (Nahal)				1984	Jordan Valley
Bracha		752	714	1982	Samaria
Dolev		880	850	1983	Benjamin
Doran				1982	Mount Hebron
Efrat	6,500	6,430	6,230	1980	Etzion Bloc
El'azar		784	747	1975	Etzion Bloc
Eli		1,900	1,730	1984	Samaria
Elisha (Nahal)		753	N/A	1983	Jordan Valley
Elkana	3,000	2,990	2,940	1977	Samaria
Elon Moreh		1,060	1,050	1979	Samaria
Emmanuel	2,700	3,040	3,150	1982	Samaria
En Hogla				1982	Jodan Valley
Enav		500	504	1981	Samaria

Eshkolot		171	148	1982	Mount Hebron
Etz Efrayim		525	500	1985	Samaria
Gannim		158	149	1983	Samaria
Geva Binyamin (Adam)		1,020	707	1983	Benjamin
Geva'ot				1984	Etzion Bloc
Gilgal		180	164	1970	Jordan Valley
Gittit		100	109	1973	Jordan Valley
Giv'at Ze'ev	10,500	10,300	10,000	1982	Benjamin
Giv'on haHadasha		1,190	1,180	1980	Benjamin
Hagai		406	405	1984	Mount Hebron
Hallamish		922	1,100	1977	Benjamin
Hamra		147	149	1971	Jordan Valley
Har Adar (Giv'at HaRadar)		1,420	1,380	1986	Benjamin
Har Gilo		369	363	1972	Etzion Bloc
Hashmona'im		1,830	1,770	1985	Benjamin
Hebron				1980	
Hemdat (Nahal)			N/A.	1980	Jordan Valley
Hermesh		279	272	1982	Samaria
Hinnanit		481	432	1981	Samaria
Homesh		159	163	1980	Samaria
Itamar		541	511	1984	Samaria
Kaddim		148	138	1983	Samaria
Kalya		260	262	1968	Jordan Valley
Karmei Zur		481	422	1984	Etzion Bloc
Karmel		246	252	1981	Mount Hebron
Karne Shomron		5,890	5,590	1978	Samaria
Kedar		447	393	1984	Benjamin
Kedumim	2,700	2,660	2,540	1975	Samaria
Kfar Adummim		1,690	1,590	1979	Benjamin
Kfar Etzion		427	421	1967	Etzion Bloc
Kfar Tapuah		347	352	1978	Samaria
Kiryat Arba'	6,400	6,380	6,240	1972	Mount Hebron

Kiryat Netafim		249	240	1982	Samaria
Kokhav haShahar		1,150	1,080	1977	Benjamin
Kokhav Ya'acov (Abir Ya'acov)		1,640	1,260	1984	Benjamin
Lapid				N/A	Benjamin
Ma'ale Adummim	25,800	24,900	23,800	1975	Benjamin
Ma'ale Amos		336	342	1981	Etzion Bloc
Ma'ale Efrayim		1,480	1,460	1970	Jordan Valley
Ma'ale Levona		445	447	1983	Benjamin
Ma'ale Mikhmas		826	753	1981	Benjamin
Ma'ale Shomron		527	486	1980	Samaria
Mahane Giv'on				1977	Benjamin
Ma'on		283	265	1981	Mount Hebron
Maskiyyot		507	N/A	1987	Jordan Valley
Massu'a		148	140	1970	Jordan Valley
Mattityahu		1,380	1,410	1981	Benjamin
Mehola		306	315	1968	Jordan Valley
Mekhora		113	120	1973	Jordan Valley
Menora		768	332	1998	Jordan Valley
Mevo Dotan		310	314	1978	Samaria
Mevo Horon		497	494	1970	Benjamin
Mezadot Yehuda		422	412	1980	Mount Hebron
Migdal Oz		289	280	1977	Etzion Bloc
Migdalim		154	150	1984	Samaria
Mizpe Shalem		210	208	1971	Megilot
Mizpe Yeriho		1,210	1,160	1978	Benjamin
Modi'in Ilit	19,200	16,400	13,000	1981	
Na'aleh		137	105	Appr./1981+	Benjamin
Nahli'el		244	230	1984	Benjamin
Negohot		409	N/A	1982	Mount Hebron
Netiv HaGedud		139	143	1976	Jordan Valley
Neve Daniyyel		933	868	1982	Etzion Bloc

Nili		721	666	1981	Benjamin
Niran		56	45	1977	Jordan Valley
Nofim		385	362	b.s.up	Samaria
Nokdim		611	526	1982	Etzion Bloc
No'omi		121	133	1982	Jordan Valley
Ofarim		686	623	1989	Benjamin
Ofra	2,000	1,880	1,870	1975	Benjamin
Oranit	5,200	5,070	4,780	1984	Samaria
Otni'el		560	553	1983	Mount Hebron
Pedu'el		885	834	1984	Samaria
Pene Hever (Ma'ale Hever)		304	266	1982	Mount Hebron
Pesagot		1,090	1,030	1981	Benjamin
Peza'el		224	228	1975	Jordan Valley
Rehan		120	100	1977	Samaria
Revava		504	389	1991	Samaria
Rimmonim		499	474	1977	Benjamin
Ro'i		141	133	1976	Jordan Valley
Rosh Zurim		265	290	1969	Etzion Bloc
Rotem (Nahal)				1984	
Sa Nur		52	54	1982	Samaria
Sal'it		410	377	1977	Samaria
Sha'are Tikva	3,500	3,380	3,220	1982	Samaria
Shadmot Mehola		399	400	1978	
Shaked		497	468	1981	Samaria
Shani		483	490	1989	Mount Hebron
Shavei Shomron		573	569	1977	Samaria
Shilo		1,580	1,490	1979	Benjamin
Shim'a		296	263	1985	Mount Hebron
Shvot Rachel				N/A	
Susiya		482	468	1983	Mount Hebron
Talmon		1,250	1,150	1989	Benjamin
Tekoa		980	948	1977	Etzion Bloc
Telem		97	101	1981	Mount Hebron
Tene (Ma'ale Omarim)		561	580	1983	Mount Hebron

Tomer		308	307	1978	Jordan Valley
Tzurif				1984	Etzion Bloc
Vered Jericho		164	155	1980	Benjamin
Ya'arit				N/A	Samaria
Yafit		125	118	1980	Jordan Valley
Yakir		822	765	1981	Samaria
Yitav		114	107	1970	Jordan Valley
Yizhar		329	328	1983	Samaria
Zufin		857	794	N/A	Samaria
Total	128,700	192,976	177,411		

Note: These data are constantly revised by the Foundation for Middle East Peace, www.fmep.org.

* *Source: List of Localities: Their Population and Codes, 31.12.1999.* Jerusalem: Central Bureau of Statistics, 2000.

** *Source: List of Localities: Their Population and Codes, 31.12.2000.* Jerusalem: Central Bureau of Statistics, 2001.

*** *Source: List of Localities: Their Population and Codes, 31.12.2001.* Jerusalem: Central Bureau of Statistics, 2002.

Glossary

'Abayah A large, loose, ankle-length overcoat that is typically made of wool for warmth. It was part of traditional Palestinian dress for men.

Abbasid Dynasty The second major Arab-Islamic dynasty based in Baghdad that ended 1258 at the hands of the Mongols.

Abu Arabic for "father (of)."

'A'ilah Arabic for "extended family."

Al-Aqsa Mosque One of two mosques built in the seventh century atop the famous plateau inside the old city of Jerusalem. It is used as an adjective of the latest Intifada (uprising) against Israeli occupation.

Al-'Ard Arabic for (social) family honor.

Al-Ard al-Muqaddasah Arabic for the Holy Land.

Al-Haram al-Sharif The Noble Sanctuary. The plateau inside the old city of Jerusalem upon which the Dome of the Rock Mosque and the al-Aqsa Mosque are built.

Al-Jaleel The Galilee hills, in northern historic Palestine and modern-day Israel.

Al-Khalil Hebron

Al-Nakba Arabic for "catastrophe," the word with which the Palestinians describe the destruction of their society in 1948 and the dispossession and expulsion of most of its people as stateless refugees.

Al-Naqab The southern desert area of historic Palestine that is shaped like an inverted north-south triangle.

Al-Quds Arabic for the Holy City, Jerusalem.

Al-Qur'an The Holy Scriptures of Islam.

'Arak A strong liquor made of distilled grape wine that is flavored with anise.

'Ataba A type of traditional song sung in the villages and rural areas of Palestine.

Ayn Jalout The Spring of Goliath in Palestine. It was the location of a battle in which the Mamluke dynasty of Egypt defeated the Mongols in Palestine.

Baba Ghannouj Mashed eggplant and sesame seed dip with spices.

Bakraj, or ibriq A small pot used to make Arabic (also called Turkish) coffee.

Baqlawa Arabic for "baklava," phyllo dough layered with crushed nuts and sweetened with syrup or honey.

Bedouins Arab or Palestinian Arab nomads.

Bir Es-Sabe' Desert town located at the northern end of al-Naqab desert. Now called Beer Sheba.

Burghul Arabic for bulgur or wheat germ.

Dal'ona A type of traditional song sung in the villages and rural areas of Palestine.

Dabke A communal dance in which the dancers, usually segregated by gender, hold hands in a semi-circle and dance to the rhythm of the music and occasionally stomp their feet in coordinated steps.

Diaspora A reference to the dispersal of the Palestinian people beyond the border of historic Palestine as result of al-Nakba.

Djillayeh The embroidered long coat with short sleeves worn over a white chemise and long pants.

Durum Durum wheat is the hard wheat produced in the hills of Palestine and exported during the nineteenth century and the early part of the twentieth century to Italy for pasta making.

'Egal Black ropes made of goat or camel hair that are used to bind the *kaffiyyeh* to the head. Part of rural Palestinian headdress for men.

Elbas Long pants that are part of traditional dress for Palestinian women.

Falafel A deep-fried small patty or ball made of ground fava beans (also called broad beans) or a mix of fava beans and chickpeas and special spices.

Firash Arabic for mattress.

Ghawr The rift valley in eastern Palestine between Lake Tiberius (the Sea of Galilee) and the Dead Sea. It is under seal level and is the lowest area on the globe.

Habkeh Binding stitch, also used in a similar fashion as the herringbone stitch but typically used for neck and sleeve openings in Palestinian embroidery.

Haifa A Palestinian city in northern Palestine, now a part of Israel.

Hakawati Traditional storyteller who often toured villages and told stories for a fee.

Hamas One of the Palestinian political factions, an Islamist political movement that has been resisting the Israeli occupation.

Hamula (pl. Hamayel) Kinship-based lineages or clans in Palestine.

Hanzala, or Hanthala The young spectator who witnesses the depicted activity in the cartoons of the artist Naji Al-'Ali that satirized a particular policy or event in the Arab world or in the Palestinian context.

Hattah *See* kaffiyyeh.

Hittin A village in Palestine near where a famous battle took place in which Saladin defeated the Crusaders in A.D. 1187.

Hummus bi-tahini A favorite Palestinian appetizer made of ground chickpeas and sesame seed dip with special spices. It is like a dip that is eaten with the flat bread and vegetables.

Ibn Arabic for "son (of)." Depending where it falls in the sentence, Ibn becomes ben or bin.

Iftar Arabic for the meal that breaks the daily fast at sundown during Ramadan.

Ilhaf Arabic for "quilt."

Innana 'Ai'doun Arabic for "we shall return." This was the first slogan of the Palestinian refugees after their expulsion from Palestine in 1948.

Intifada Arabic term for an uprising that is used to describe the Palestinian uprisings against Israeli occupation.

Jabal Al-Khalil Mount Hebron in southeastern Palestine.

Jabal al-Quds Mount Jerusalem in central Palestine.

Jabal Nablus Mount Nablus in north-central Palestine.

Jaffa The historical port city of central Palestine that gave its name to the famous Palestinian oranges. It is now a mixed Arab-Jewish city that has become the coastal suburb of Tel Aviv in modern-day Israel.

Jibneh Arabic for "cheese."

Jund Filastin Arabic for the district of Palestine in the first Arab-Islamic Empire.

Kabab Kabobs; meat cooked on a skewer.

Kaffiyyeh The square piece of cloth (with or without design) that forms the Palestinian headdress of rural men in Palestine.

Khubz Arabic for "bread." The type of flat bread that is known in the United States as pita bread.

Kibbi Ground meat mixed with spices and bulgar wheat and cooked in a variety of ways (e.g., fried, baked, or grilled).

Kibbi Nayyi Kibbi that is not cooked but eaten like steak tartar with spices.

Knafi Nabulsiyyeh A sweet dessert famous in the city of Nablus. It is made of soft, unsalted cheese covered with a shredded wheat.

Labaneh A paste of soft cheese made from yogurt that has the whey drained from it.

Laffeh A cloth wrap that forms a turban. Worn by Palestinian men and some functionaries.

Mahshi (pl. Mahashi) The generic name for all stuffed dishes including stuffed squash, eggplants tomatoes, and green peppers.

Malak Meaning "queenly," the name of the traditional embroidered wedding dress or costume that a bride proudly wears on her wedding day.

Mamlukes A slave dynasty that ruled Egypt for about 250 years until 1517. The Mamlukes controlled Palestine, which they acquired after they defeated the Mongol invaders.

Maqloubeh Arabic for up side down. The name for a type of rice, vegetable, and meat dish. Rice is layered with meat and vegetables, such as cauliflower or eggplant, at the bottom of the cooking pot, which is turned upside-down when served at the table.

Marj Ibn 'Amer The name of the fertile valley that bisects historic Palestine in the center and separates Mount Jerusalem from the Galilee hills.

Marqouq A thin Palestinian bread that is baked over a metal dome on an open fire.

Mazboutah or Wasat Arabic terms that means "just right." It is a reference to the degree of sweetness that Arabic or Turkish coffee should have.

Mazza An elaborate and large variety of appetizers including many hot and cold dishes served in small number in homes before a meal or as side dishes in large numbers at restaurants.

Minbar A pulpit in a mosque.

Moa'akhar The amount of money or assets that is due to the wife from the husband in case of a divorce. The amount for the mo'akhar can be symbolic or extensive as the two parties wish. There is no specific money exchanged for the mo'akhar at the time of engagement or marriage.

Mughli A pudding made of semolina wheat, sweetened with sugar, flavored with cinnamon, and topped with fresh nuts, especially almonds with their brown skins removed. It is typically served upon the birth of a new child.

Muhur Dowry given to the bride by her future husband. The dowry is set in accordance with the social status of the two principals.

Nabatean Arabs A pre-Christian and pre-Islamic Arab people who were traders and who built a kingdom that stretched from northwestern modern day Saudi Arabia, through southwestern Jordan, into historic southern Palestine. They are most famous for the beautiful and incredible city they built in Jordan called Petra.

Omayyad Dynasty The second Arab-Islamic dynasty.

Qadi A Sunni Muslim religious judge.

Qahwi Arabic for "coffee."

Qamis Arabic for "chemise" or "shirt."

Qarawi Traditional hand-loomed cotton fabric made in Palestinian villages.

Qumbaz A traditional tunic worn by Palestinian villagers.

Roumi Handloomed linen on which embroidery is sown.

Sabaleh Herringbone stitch used to join seams, for framing appliqué, and for embellishing and reinforcing hems in Palestinian embroidery.

Sahtayn "Two healths." Similar to the French phrase *bon appetite* except it is said after the meal is finished rather than before.

Salah Ed-Deen Saladin in English. The Islamic commander who defeated the Crusaders in the battle of Hittin in Palestine in 1187.

Salatat al-Bandura Arabic for "tomato salad."

Samed The economic and investment arm of the Palestine Liberation Organization in Lebanon.

Sfiha A triangular- or square-shaped doughpocket filled with vegetables or labaneh; eaten as an appetizer.

Sharab, Shurbat (pl. Sharabat) A refreshing drink prepared with cold water flavored with sweet syrups made from fruit nectars such as pomegranate, mulberry, and others.

Sharaf Family honor defined narrowly as residing in the women of the family, who are expected to exhibit modesty in demeanor and dress, self-restraint, self-effacement, sexual chastity before marriage, fidelity after, and obedience to male guardians, husbands, and elders.

Shawurma Arabic for gyro meat dishes. A popular "fast food."

Shirwal Traditional baggy pants worn by peasants in Palestine.

Tabbouli A salad made of minced or diced parsley with bulgar wheat, lemon juice, olive oil, and salt and pepper; certain regions add additional spices.

Tahini A flavoring paste or sauce made of sesame seeds. It is one of the principal ingredient in hummus, baba ghannouj, and many other dishes.

Taqsirah Short embroidered jacket traditionally worn by Palestinian women.

Tarator A sauce for fish made from tahini and seasoned with lemon juice and spices.

Tarbush A red fez, of Turkish origin, worn by urban Palestinians of the middle class before the collapse of the Ottoman Empire in 1917.

Ummah The term that the Prophet Muhammad gave to the new Muslim community he had founded. In contemporary Arabic, it also means nation.

Wadi Araba The name of the valley and geological rift south of the Dead Sea, which constitutes the southern border between Jordan and modern Israel.

Za'atar Thyme, a favorite Palestinian herb. It is mixed with olive oil, spread on a piece of dough, and cooked like a pizza.

Zaghareet A type of traditional song typically sung by women in the villages and rural areas of Palestine.

Zajal A type of traditional poetry and song recited and sung in the villages and rural areas of Palestine often by itinerant zajjalin.

Zajjal (pl. Zajjalin) Traditional itinerant singer and poetry reader who is paid a fee both in kind and cash.

Zalabi, or Luqmat al-Qadi A deep-fried pastry that is like a light, crisp doughnut typically served during holidays.

Zionism A political movement that emerged in Europe among Jewish communities whose purpose was to solve the dilemma of European anti-Semitism. It proposed to remove European Jewery to a colonial settlement outside Europe. Inspired by nineteenth century European colonialism, Zionism proposed to colonize Arab Palestine as the national home for the Jews.

Bibliography

GENERAL REFERENCES

Abdul-Hadi, Mahdi F., ed. *Palestine: Documents*. 2 vols. Jerusalem: PASSIA, 1997.

Applied Research Institute. *An Atlas of Palestine*. Bethlehem: Applied Research Institute, 2000.

Ingrams, Doreen, compiler. *Palestine Papers 1917–1922: Seeds of Conflict*. New York: George Braziller, 1973.

Institute for Palestine Studies, ed. *United Nations Resolutions on Palestine and the Arab-Israeli Conflict*, 5 vols. Washington, DC: Institute for Palestine Studies.

Mattar, Philip, ed. *Encyclopedia of the Palestinians*. New York: Facts on File, 2000.

Nakhleh, Issa. *Encyclopedia of the Palestine Problem*, 2 vols. New York: Intercontinental Books, 1991.

Nazzal, Nafez, and Laila Nazzal. *Historical Dictionary of Palestine*. Lanham, MD: Scarecrow Press, 1997.

GENERAL READINGS

Farsoun, Samih, with Christina Zacharia. *Palestine and the Palestinians*. Boulder, CO: Westview Press, 1997.

Finkelstein, Norman. *The Rise and Fall of Palestine*. Minneapolis: University of Minnesota Press, 1996.

Hiro, Dilip. *Sharing the Promised Land: A Tale of Israelis and Palestinians*. New York: Olive Branch Press, 1999, 1996.

Kapitan, Tomis, ed. *Philosophical Perspectives on the Israeli-Palestinian Conflict*. Armonk, NY: Sharpe, 1997.

Khalidi, Walid. *Palestine Reborn*. New York: I.B. Tauris, 1992.

Kimmerling, Baruch, and Joel S. Migdal. *The Palestinian People: A History*. Cambridge: Harvard University Press, 2003.

Rodinson, Maxine. *Israel: A Colonial-Settler State?* New York: Monad Press, 1973.

Said, Edward. *The Question of Palestine*. New York: Vintage, 1980.

Sharabi, Hisham. *Palestine and Israel: The Lethal Dilemma*. New York: Pegasus, 1969.

HISTORY

Premodern History

Thompson, Thomas. *The Mythic Past: Biblical Archaeology and the Myth of Israel*. London: Basic Books, 1999.

Whitelam, Keith W. *The Invention of Ancient Israel: The Silencing of Palestinian History*. New York: Routledge, 1996.

Pre-1948

Doumani, Beshara. *Rediscovering Palestine: Merchants and Peasants in Jabal Nablus, 1700–1900*. Berkeley: University of California Press, 1995.

Huneidi, Sahar. *A Broken Trust: Herbert Samuel, Zionism and the Palestinians, 1920–1925*. New York: Tauris, 2001.

Khalidi, Walid. *Before Their Diaspora: A Photographic History of the Palestinians, 1876–1948*. Washington, DC: Institute for Palestine Studies, 1991.

Masalha, Nur. *Expulsion of the Palestinians: The Concept of "Transfer" in Zionist Political Thought, 1882–1948*. Washington, DC: Institute for Palestine Studies, 1992.

Mattar, Phillip. *The Mufti of Jerusalem* New York: Columbia University Press, 1992.

Muslih, Muhammad Y. *The Origins of Palestinian Nationalism*. New York: Columbia University Press, 1988.

Owen, Roger, ed. *Studies in the Economic History of Palestine in the Nineteenth and Twentieth Centuries*. Carbondale: Southern Illinois University Press, 1982.

Scholch, Alexander. *Palestine in Transformation, 1856–1882: Studies in Social, Economic and Political Development*. Washington, DC: Institute for Palestine Studies, 1993.

Shafir, Gershon. *Land, Labor, and the Origins of the Israeli-Palestinian Conflict, 1882–1914*. New York: Cambridge University Press, 1989.

Smith, Barbara. *The Roots of Separatism in Palestine, British Economic Policy, 1920–1929*. Syracuse, NY: Syracuse University Press, 1993.

Stevens, Georgiana G. *Jordan River Partition*. Stanford, CA: Hoover Institute, 1965.

Swedenberg, Ted. *Memories of Revolt: The 1936–1939 Rebellion and the Palestinian National Past*. Minneapolis: University of Minnesota Press, 1995.

Post-1948

Abu-Lughod, Ibrahim, ed. *The Transformation of Palestine*. Evanston: Northwestern University Press, 1971.

Hadawi, Sami. *Palestinian Rights and Losses in 1948: A Comprehensive Study*. London: Saqi Books, 1988.

Khalidi, Walid. *All That Remains: The Palestinian Villages Occupied and Depopulated by Israel in 1948*. Washington, DC: Institute for Palestine Studies, 1992.

McGowan, Daniel, and Marc Ellis. *Remembering Deir Yassin: The Future of Israel and Palestine*. New York: Olive Branch Press, 1998.

Palumbo, Michael. *The Palestinian Catastrophe: The 1948 Expulsion of a People from Their Homeland*. New York: Olive Branch Press, 1991.

Pappe, Ilan. *The Making of the Arab-Israel Conflict, 1947–1951*. London: Tauris, 1992.

Tamari, Salim. *Jerusalem 1948: The Arab Neighborhoods and Their Fate in the War*. Jerusalem: Institute of Jerusalem Studies and Badil Resource Center, 1999.

Toubbeh, Jamil I. *Day of the Long Night: A Palestinian Refugee Remembers the Nakba*. Jefferson, NC: McFarland, 1997.

Zurayk, Constantine K. *The Meaning of the Disaster*. Translated by R. B. Winder. Beirut: Khayat's College Book Cooperative, 1956.

Palestinian Refugees

Aruri, Naseer, ed. *Palestinian Refugees: The Right of Return*. Sterling, VA: Pluto Press, 2001.

Karmi, Ghada, Eugene Cotran, and Ian Gilmour. *The Palestinian Exodus, 1948–1998*. London: Ithaca Press, 2000.

Peretz, Don. *Palestinians, Refugees, and the Middle East Peace Process*. Washington, DC: United States Institute of Peace, 1993.

POLITICS

Palestinian Politics

Ateek, Naim. *Justice and Only Justice: A Palestinian Theology of Liberation*. Maryknoll, NY: Orbis Books, 1989.

Brand, Laurie. *Palestinians in the Arab World*. New York: Columbia University Press, 1988.

Brynen, Rex. *Sanctuary and Survival: The PLO in Lebanon*. Boulder, CO: Westview Press, 1990.

Bunzl, John, and Benjamin Beit-Hallahmi, eds. *Psychoanalysis, Identity, and Ideology: Critical Essays on the Israel/Palestine Case*. Boston: Kluwer Academic, 2002.

Elmusa, Sharif. *Water Conflict: Economics, Politics, Law and Palestinian-Israeli Water Resources*. Washington, DC: Institute for Palestine Studies, 1997.

Gresh, Alain. *The PLO: The Struggle Within*. London: Zed Press, 1985.

Hart, Alan. *Arafat: A Political Biography*. London: Sidgwick & Jackson, 1994.

Hudson, Michael, ed. *The Palestinians: New Directions*. Washington, DC: Center for Contemporary Arab Studies, 1990.

Muslih, Mohammad. *The Origins of Palestinian Nationalism*. New York: Columbia University Press, 1988.

Quandt, William, et al. *The Politics of Palestinian Nationalism*. Berkeley: University of California Press, 1973.

Robinson, Glenn E. *Building a Palestinian State: The Incomplete Revolution*. Bloomington: Indiana University Press, 1997.

Sayigh, Rosemary. *Too Many Enemies*. London: Zed Books, 1994.

Sayigh, Yezid. *Armed Struggle and the Search for State: The Palestinian National Movement, 1949–1993*. New York: Oxford University Press, 1997.

U.S. Role

Aruri, Naseer. *The Obstruction of Peace: The U.S., Israel, and the Palestinians*. Monroe, ME: Common Courage Press, 1995.

Aruri, Naseer H. *Dishonest Broker: The U.S. Role in Israel and Palestine*. Cambridge, MA: South End Press, 2003.

Chomsky, Noam. *Fateful Triangle: The United States, Israel, and the Palestinians*. Cambridge, MA: South End Press, 1999.

Christison, Kathleen. *Perceptions of Palestine*. Berkeley: University of California Press, 1999.

The Conflict and the Peace Process

Abbas, Mahmud. *Through Secret Channels: The Road to Oslo*. Reading, PA: Garnet, 1995.

Ashrawi, Hanan. *This Side of Peace*. New York: Simon and Schuster, 1995.

Bishara, Marwan. *Palestine/Israel: Peace or Apartheid*. New York: Zed Books, 2001.

Cohen, Avner. *Israel and the Bomb*. New York: Columbia University Press, 1998.

Finkelstein, Norman. *Image and Reality of the Israel-Palestine Conflict*. London: Verso, 1993.

Gee, John R. *Unequal Conflict: The Palestinians and Israel*. New York: Olive Branch Press, 1998.

Giacaman, George, and Dag Jorund Lonning. *After Oslo: New Realities, Old Problems*. Chicago: Pluto Press, 1998.

Guyatt, Nicholas. *The Absence of Peace: Understanding the Israeli-Palestinian Conflict*. New York: Zed Books, 1998.

Mallison, W. T., and S. V. Mallison. *The Role of International Law in Achieving Justice and Peace in Palestine-Israel*. New York: Americans for Middle East Understanding, 1974.

Pappe, Ilan, ed. *The Israel/Palestine Question*. New York: Routledge, 1999.

Peretz, Don. *The Arab-Israeli Dispute*. New York: Facts on File, 1996.

Reinhart, Tanya. *Israel/Palestine: How to End the War of 1948*. New York: Seven Stories Press, 2002.

Quandt, William. *Peace Process*. Washington, DC, and Berkeley: Brookings Institute and University of California Press, 1993.

Said, Edward. *The Politics of Dispossession: The Struggle of Palestinian Self-Determination, 1969–1994*. New York: Pantheon, 1994.

Said, Edward. *Peace and Its Discontents: Essays on Palestine in the Middle East*. New York: Vintage, 1995.

Shahak, Israel. *Open Secrets: Israeli Foreign and Nuclear Policies*. Chicago: Pluto Press, 1997.

Usher, Graham. *Palestine in Crisis: The Struggle for Peace and Political Independence after Oslo*. East Haven, CT: Pluto Press, 1995.

OCCUPIED PALESTINIAN TERRITORIES

Abu Amr, Ziyad. *Islamic Fundamentalism in the West Bank and Gaza: Muslim Brotherhood and Islamic Jihad*. Bloomington: Indiana University Press, 1994.

Aburish, Said K. *Cry Palestine: Inside the West Bank*. Boulder, CO: Westview Press, 1993.

Amery, Hussein A., and Aaron T. Wolf, eds. *Water in the Middle East: A Geography of Peace*. Austin: University of Texas Press, 2000.

Aronson, Geoffrey. *Israel, Palestinians, and the Intifada: Creating Facts on the West Bank*. New York: Kegan Paul, 1990.

Aruri, Naseer, ed. *Occupation: Israel over Palestine*. Belmont, MA: Association of Arab American University Graduates, 1989.

Baroud, Ramzy, ed. *Searching Jenin: Eyewitness Accounts of the Israeli Invasion*. Seattle, WA: Cune Press, 2003.

Brynen, Rex, ed. *Echoes of the Intifada: Regional Repercussions of the Palestinian-Israeli Conflict*. Boulder, CO: Westview Press, 1991.

Carey, Roaneed. *The New Intifada: Resisting Israel's Apartheid*. New York: Verso, 2001.

Chacham, Ronit. *Breaking Ranks: Refusing to Serve in the West Bank and Gaza Strip*. New York: Other Press, 2003.

Chacour, Elias. *We Belong to the Land: The Story of a Palestinian Israeli Who Lives for Peace and Reconciliation*. San Francisco: Harper, 1992.

Chesin, Amir S., Bill Hutman, and Avi Melamed. *Separate and Unequal: The Inside Story of Israeli Rule in East Jerusalem*. Cambridge: Harvard University Press, 1999.

Doughty, Dick, and Mohammed El Aydi. *Gaza Legacy of Occupation: A Photographer's Journey*. West Hartford: Kumarian Press, 1995.

Dumper, Michael. *The Politics of Jerusalem since 1967*. New York: Columbia University Press, 1997.

Dumper, Michael. *Islam and Israel: Muslim Religious Endowments and the Jewish State*. Washington, DC: Institute for Palestine Studies, 1994.

Ghanem, As'ad. *The Palestinian-Arab Minority in Israel, 1948–2000: A Political Study*. Albany: State University of New York Press, 2001.

Gunn, Janet Varner. *A Second Life: A West Bank Memoir*. Minneapolis: University of Minnesota Press, 1995.

Hamzeh, Muna, and Todd May, eds. *Operation Defensive Shield: Witnesses to Israeli War Crimes*. Sterling, VA: Pluto Press, 2003.

Hass, Amira. *Drinking the Sea at Gaza: Days and Nights in a Land Under Siege*. New York: Henry Holt, 1999.

Heiberg, Marianne. *Palestinian Society in Gaza, West Bank and Arab Jerusalem: A Survey of Living Conditions*. Oslo: FAFO, 1993.

Hilterman, Joost. *Behind the Intifada: Labor and Women's Movements in the Occupied Territories*. Princeton: Princeton University Press, 1991.

Hoffman, Michael, and Moshe Lieberman. *The Israeli Holocaust against the Palestinians*. Coeur d'Alene, ID: Independent History, 2002.

Kimmerling, Baruch. *Politicide: Ariel Sharon's War against the Palestinians*. New York: Verso, 2003.

Lustick, Ian. *Arabs in the Jewish State: Israel's Control of a National Minority*. Austin: University of Texas Press, 1980.

Monk, Daniel Bertrand. *An Aesthetic Occupation: The Immediacy of Architecture and the Palestine Conflict*. Durham, NC: Duke University Press, 2002.

Nuseibeh, Said. *The Dome of the Rock*. New York: Rizzoli, 1996.

Rouhana, Nadim. *Palestinian Citizens in an Ethnic Jewish State*. New Haven, CT: Yale University Press, 1997.

Roy, Sara M. *The Gaza Strip: The Political Economy of De-Development*. Washington, DC: Institute for Palestine Studies, 1995.

Shehadeh, Raja. *Israel and the West Bank*. Washington, DC: Institute for Palestine Studies, 1988.

Tamari, Salim. *Jerusalem 1948: The Arab Neighborhoods and Their Fate in the War*. Jerusalem: Institute of Jerusalem Studies and Badil Resource Center, 1999.

Zureik, Elia. *The Palestinians in Israel: A Study in Internal Colonialism*. London: Routledge & Kegan Paul, 1979.

ECONOMICS AND POLITICAL ECONOMY

Abed, George T. *The Economic Viability of a Palestinian State*. Washington, DC: Institute for Palestine Studies, 1990.

Brynen, Rex. *The (Very) Political Economy of the West Bank and Gaza: Learning Lessons about Peace-Building and Development Assistance*. Washington, DC: United States Institute of Peace, 2000.

Diwan, Ishac, and Radwan Shaban. *Development under Adversity: The Palestinian Economy*. Washington, DC: World Bank, 1999.

Khalidi, Raja. *The Arab Economy in Israel: The Dynamics of a Region's Development*. London: Routledge & Kegan Paul, 1988.

WOMEN AND GENDER

Kanaaneh, Rhoda Ann. *Birthing the Nation: Strategies of Palestinian Women in Israel*. Berkeley: University of California Press, 2002.

Kawar, Amal. *Daughters of Palestine*. Albany: State University of New York Press, 1996.

Mayer, Tamar, ed. *Women and the Israeli Occupation: The Politics of Change*. New York: Routledge, 1994.

Najjar, Orayb Aref. *Portraits of Palestinian Women*. Salt Lake City: University of Utah Press, 1992.

Peteet, Julie. *Gender in Crisis: Women and the Palestinian Resistance Movement*. New York: Columbia University Press, 1991.

Rubenberg, Cheryl. *Palestinian Women, Patriarchy and Resistance in the West Bank*. Boulder, CO: Lynne Rienner, 2001.

Sabbagh, Suha, ed. *Palestinian Women of Gaza and the West Bank*. Bloomington: Indiana University Press, 1998.

Sharoni, Simona. *Gender and the Israeli-Palestinian Conflict*. Syracuse, NY: Syracuse University Press, 1995.

PALESTINIAN CULTURE AND SOCIETY

Abu-Ghazaleh, Adnan. *Palestinian Arab Cultural Nationalism*. Brattleboro, VT: Amana Books, 1991.

Elad-Bouskila, Ami. *Modern Palestinian Literature and Culture*. Portland, OR: Cass, 1999.

El-Khalidi, Leila. *The Art of Palestinian Embroidery*. London: Saqi Books, 1999.

Jayyusi, Salma Khadra, ed. *Anthology of Modern Palestinian Literature*. New York: Columbia University Press, 1992.

Muhawi, Ibrahim, and Sharif Kanaana, eds. *Speak, Bird, Speak Again: Palestinian Arab Folktales*. Berkeley: University of California Press, 1989.

Rajab, Jehan. *Palestinian Costume*. New York: Ruteledge, Chapman, and Hall, 1989.

Tordai, J. C., and Graham Usher. *A People Called Palestine*. London: Dewi Lewis, 2001.

Weir, Shelagh. *Palestinian Costume*. London: British Museum, 1989.

ZIONISM

Avineri, Shlomo. *The Making of Modern Zionism: Intellectual Origins of the Jewish State*. New York: Basic Books, 1981.

Ben-Menashe, Ari. *Profits of War: Inside the Secret U.S.-Israeli Arms Network*. New York: Sheridan Square Press, 1992.

Brenner, Lenni. *Zionism in the Age of Dictators*. Westport, CT: Hill, 1983.

Brenner, Lenni. *The Iron Wall: Zionist Revisionism from Jabotinsky to Shamir*. Totowa, NJ: Palgrave Macmillan1984.

Finkelstein, Norman G. *The Holocaust Industry: Reflections on the Exploitation of Jewish Suffering*. New York: Verso, 2000.

Heller, Joseph. *The Stern Gang: Ideology, Politics and Terror, 1940–1949*. Portland, OR: Frank Cass, 1995.

Mezvinsky, Norton, and Israel Shahak. *Jewish Fundamentalism in Israel*. Sterling, VA: Pluto Press, 1999.

Nicosia, Francis R. *The Third Reich and the Palestine Question*. New Brunswick, NJ: Transaction, 2000.

Peled, Yoav, and Gershon Shafir. *Being Israeli: The Dynamics of Multiple Citizenship*. New York: Cambridge University Press, 2002.

Segev, Tom. *The Seventh Million: The Israelis and the Holocaust*, translated by Haim Watzman. New York: Henry Holt, 1991.

Shapiro, Yonathan. *The Road to Power: Herut Party in Israel*, translated by Ralph Mandel. Albany: State University of New York Press, 1991.

Sharon, Ariel, and David Chanoff. *Warrior: An Autobiography*. New York: Touchstone, 2001 (1989).

Shindler, Colin. *The Land Beyond Promise: Israel, Likud and the Zionist Dream*. New York: Tauris, 2002.

Sprinzak, Ehud. *The Ascendance of Israel's Radical Right*. New York: Oxford University Press, 1991.

Thomas, Gordan. *Gideon's Spies: The Secret History of the Mossad*. New York: St. Martin's Press, 1999.

GENERAL: ARAB WORLD

Anderson, Lisa, et al. *The Origins of Arab Nationalism*. New York: Columbia University Press, 1993.

Barakat, Halim. *The Arab World: Society, Culture, and State*. Berkeley: University of California Press, 1993.

Hourani, Albert. *A History of the Arab Peoples*. New York: Warner Books, 1991.

RECOMMENDED PERIODICALS ON PALESTINE

Between the Lines

Challenge
Journal of Palestine Studies
News from Within
Palestine-Israel Journal

MIDDLE EAST PERIODICALS THAT DEAL WITH PALESTINE

Arab Studies Quarterly
The Middle East Journal
Middle East Policy
Middle East Report
Washington Report on Middle East Affairs

EDUCATIONAL INSTITUTIONS

Universities

Al Azhar University of Gaza, http://www.alazhar-gaza.edu
Al-Quds University, http://www.alquds.edu
An-Najah National University, http://www.najah.edu
Bethlehem University, http://www.bethlehem.edu
Birzeit University, http://www.birzeit.edu
Islamic University of Gaza, http://www.iugaza.edu

Research Institutes and Centers

Al-Multaqa: Arab Thought Forum, http://www.multaqa.org
The Galilee Society: The Arab National Society for Health Research and Services, http://www.gal-soc.org
Hebron Institute for Political and Religious Studies, http://www.hebron.org
Institute for Palestine Studies, http://www.ipsjps.org
Jerusalem Media and Communications Center, http://www.jmcc.org
MUWATIN: The Palestinian Institute For the Study of Democracy, http://www.muwatin.org
Oxford University: Refugee Studies Center, http://www.qeh.ox.ac.uk/rsp/indexrsp
The Palestine Center, http://www.palestinecenter.org
Palestinian Academic Society for the Study of International Affairs, http://www.passia.org
Palestinian Center for Peace and Democracy, http://www.pcpd.org
Palestinian Refugee ResearchNet at McGill University, http://www.arts.mcgill.ca/MEPP/PRRN
Shaml: The Palestinian Diaspora and Refugee Centre, http://www.shaml.org
Trans-Arab Research Institute, http://www.tari.org

GOVERNMENTAL SITES

NGO Network on the Question of Palestine, http://www.un.org/Depts/dpa/ngo
Palestinian Central Bureau of Statistics, http://www.pcbs.org

Palestinian National Authority, http://www.pna.gov.ps
UN Relief and Works Agency, http://www.un.org/unrwa
UNDP: Program of Assistance to the Palestinian People, http://www.papp.undp.org
USAID: West Bank and Gaza Mission, http://www.usaid.gov/wbg

GOVERNMENTAL ORGANIZATIONS

In Palestine and Israel

Adalah: The Legal Center for Arab Minority Rights in Israel, http://www.adalah.org
"Addameer" Prisoners Support and Human Rights Association, http://www.addameer.org
Al-Haq: West Bank affiliate of the Geneva-based International Commission of Jurists,
      http://www.alhaq.org
BADIL: Resource Center for Palestinian Residency and Refugee Rights, http://www.
      badil.org
The Birzeit University Human Rights Action Project, http://www.birzeit.edu/hrap
B'Tselem: The Israeli Information Center for Human Rights in the Occupied Territories,
      http://www.btselem.org
Defense for Children International/Palestine Section, http://www.dci-pal.org
Dheisheh Refugee Camp, http://www.dheisheh-ibdaa.org
Health, Development, Information, and Policy Institute, HDIP, http://www.hdip.org
Israeli Committee Against House Demolitions, http://www.icahd.org
Ittijah: Union of Arab Community Based Associations, http://www.ittijah.org
Jerusalemites, http://www.jerusalemites.org
The Jerusalem Center for Women, http://www.j-c-w.org
LAW: The Palestinian Society for the Protection of Human Rights & the Environment,
      http://www.lawsociety.org
MIFTAH: The Palestinian Initiative for the Promotion of Global Dialogue & Democracy,
      http://www.miftah.org
Palestinian Human Rights Monitoring Group, http://www.phrmg.org
Palestinian Center for Human Rights, http://www.pchrgaza.org
The Palestinian Independent Commission for Citizens' Rights, http://www.piccr.org
Palestinian Non-Governmental Organizations Network, http://www.pngo.net
Palestine Red Crescent Society, http://www.palestinecrs.org
Palestinian Rights Programme of the Foreign & Commonwealth Office, http://www.
      palestine-rights.org
Palestinian Working Woman Society for Development, http://www.pal-pwws.org
Rawdat El-Zuhur, http://www.rawdat.org
Sunbula, http://www.sunbula.org
Wi'am Center-Palestinian Conflict Resolution Center, http://www.planet.edu
Women's Affairs Technical Committee, http://www.palwatc.org

Outside Palestine

Al Nakba, http://www.alnakba.org
American Federation of Ramallah, Palestine, http://www.afrp.org
American Near East Refugee Aid, http://www.anera.org
American Palestine Political Education Committee, http://www.appec.com

Americans and Palestinians for Peace, http://www.muscanet.com
Arab American Institute, http://www.aaiusa.org
Arab Community Center for Economic and Social Services, http://www.comnet.org
Council for the National Interest, http://www.cnionline.org
Council for Palestinian Restitution and Repatriation, http://www.rightofreturn.org
Deir Yassin Remembered, http://www.deiryassin.org
Foundation for Middle East Peace, http://www.fmep.org
International Solidarity Movement, http://www.rapprochement.org
Jews against the Occupation, http://www.jewsagainsttheoccupation.org
Madre, http://www.madre.org/country_pal.html
Middle East Children's Alliance, http://www.mecaforpeace.org
Middle East Policy Council, http://www.mepc.org
The Middle East Research and Information Project, http://www.merip.org
Palestine Remembered, http://www.palestineremembered.org
Palestinian Eye, http://www.paleye.net
Sabra and Shatila, http://www.sabra-shatila.org

MEDIA

Newspapers

Al-Quds Newspaper, http://www.alquds.com
Al Sabar, http://www.odaction.org/alsabar
Assabeel Weekly, http://www.assabeel.org
Ha'aretz Daily, Internet Edition, http://www.haaretzdaily.com
Palestine Times, http://www.ptimes.com

Magazines and Journals

Al Bawaba: The Middle East Gateway, http://www.albawaba.com
Forced Migration Review, http://www.fmreview.org
InfoPal: The Independent Palestinian Information Network, http://www.infopal.org
Jerusalem Quarterly File, http://www.jqf-jerusalem.org
Middle East Policy, http://www.mepc.org
Palestine Chronicle, http://www.palestinechronicle.com
The Palestine Monitor: The Voice of Civil Society, http://www.palestinemonitor.org
Palestine Report, http://www.jmcc.org/media/reportonline
A Personal Diary of the Israeli-Palestinian Conflict, http://www.nigel parry.com/diary
Washington Report on Middle East Affairs, http://www.washington-report.org

RELIGIOUS ORGANIZATIONS

Al Bushra: Arab-American Roman Catholic Community, http://www.al-bushra.org
American Friends Service Committee, http://www.afsc.org
Christian Peacemaker Teams, http://www.prairienet.org/cpt
Churches for Middle East Peace, http://www.cmep.org
Evangelicals for Middle East Understanding, http://www.campus.nothpark.edu/centers/
    middle.emeu

Menonite Central Community, http://www.mcc.org/areaserv/middleeast/palestine/index.
    html
Methodist Federation for Social Action, http://www.mfsaweb.org
The Middle East Council of Churches, http://www.mecchurches.org
Sabeel: Ecumenical Liberation Theology Center, http://www.sabeel.org

CULTURAL SITES

Al-Jana: The Arab Resource Center for Popular Arts, http://www.oneworld.org/al-jana
Al-Karmel, http://www.alkarmel.org
Ashtar Theatre, http://www.ashtar-theatre.org
House of Poetry—The Palestinian Cultural Center, http://www.pal-poetry.org
Khalil Sakakini Cultural Center, http://www.sakakini.org
Occupied Territory, http://www.occupied.org
The Palestine Poster Project, http://www.liberationgraphics.com/palestine.html
Riwaq: Center for Architectural Conservation, http://www.riwaq.org
Sindibad Films, http://www.sindibad.co.uk
Yafa Cultural Center, http://www.palnet.com/%7Eyafa

Index

About the Author

SAMIH K. FARSOUN is Dean of Academic Affairs and the College of Arts and Sciences at the American University in Kuwait.